THE GATEFOLD BOOK OF THE WORLD

WARSHIPS

BROWN BOOKS

First published in Great Britain in 1994 by
Brown Books, 255-257 Liverpool Road, London N1 1LX

ISBN 1-897884-02-8

Printed by Vincenzo Bona, Torino, Italy

CONTENTS

INTRODUCTION

ABOVE: An aerial shot of an Iowa-class battleship records the effect on the neighbourhood of a broadside from nine 406mm (15.9in) guns. The four completed Iowas were commissioned in 1943/44 and have had long careers, being deactivated and reactivated according to need. Two of the class took part in the Gulf War of 1991, but by 1992 all four were once again in reserve.

From the first, ships and boats have had two purposes: peaceful trade on the one hand, warfare in some shape or form on the other. There have been times when a single vessel was supposed to combine both tasks, but the result was never completely satisfactory – there is just too much difference between the warship and the merchantman for a hybrid to stand much real chance of success in either role. Merchant ships are fat and cumbersome in general; men-o'-war are leaner and fitter.

The seafaring peoples of the Mediterranean all recognised this, and built distinctly different ships for the two jobs. The various cultures evidently learned from each other, and we see the development of the oared warship from the Phoenician ships of Tyre and Sidon, through the very similar vessels the Greeks built, to the Roman trireme,

certainly the most fearsome war machine pre-Christian man had ever seen.

It was the nature of the environment, as much as anything, that channelled naval development in the Mediterranean – the region's rapidly changing wind patterns meant that the more predictable oared warship continued in use there long after it had gone out of fashion elsewhere (except in the shallow waters of the Baltic, where different conditions apply). Of course, oared warships were not unique to the Mediterranean, and one other type in particular – the Viking longship – almost symbolises the Dark Ages between the fall of Rome and the Renaissance.

When European civilisation declined after the fall of Rome, ship development generally stagnated and didn't really get moving again until the 14th century, but then developments of all sorts came in a

rush. The hull form of the sailing ship, for instance, became longer in relation to the width of the beam. Previously the biggest difference between the shape of merchant sailing ships and oared warships was in their proportions. The merchant ships were 'round', while the longships and galleys were up to six times as long as they were wide. Now, the merchant sailing ship changed to proportions of around three to one, and when the warship lost its oars and came to depend on sail alone, it took a similar form.

Other developments around this time included the adoption of the centre-line rudder in place of the steering oars mounted on the quarters, which improved controllability, and the introduction of a second mast, right forward, which improved sailing performance. By the middle of the 15th century, a third mast –

the mizzen – had been added on the quarter-deck aft, and this mounted a lateen fore-and-aft sail. It only remained to add topmasts and topsails, and the full-rigged sailing ship would be born.

THE ADVENT OF THE GUN

Arguably the most significant step in the evolution of the warship of the period, however, was the development of the gun. Though guns had gone to sea before the 14th century was half-way over, it was not until the early 15th century that they came to be regarded as a significant part of a warship's armament. It was fully five decades more before they were incorporated in anything like substantial numbers. At this point they were still quite small-calibre pieces mostly, sited in the fore- and aftercastles. By the end of the century, however, we find sailing warships with much bigger guns in the waist, arranged to fire in broadside. The oared warships that persisted in the Mediterranean, especially the biggest, such as the royal galley of the Christian commander-in-chief at the battle of Lepanto, Don John of Austria, acquired very large guns, too. These were mounted in the bow, flanked by a pair or two of smaller pieces, and arranged to fire forwards. There was, in fact, nowhere else to mount the guns in a galley, since the rowing benches occupied the entire broadside space, and that was the final nail in the vessel's coffin. Lepanto, in 1571, was the last occasion on which large fleets of oared warships met.

Before the appearance of guns, a major role of the warship had been as a fighting platform for infantry and archers, and this led them to be provided with 'castles' – fighting towers – at bow and stern, to give soldiers a height advantage. At first these were temporary structures, but later they became permanent and an accepted feature. The high forecastle endured until the second half of the 16th century, when there was a quite sudden change from 'high charged' carracks, with towering structures overhanging the bow, to 'low charged' galleons, with a forecastle deck only slightly raised above the waist. The reward was much improved performance to windward.

Soon, ships were being built with a length-to-beam ratio of 4:1 – a typical large late-16th century galleon, such as the Duke of Medina-Sidonia's 'Invincible Armada' flagship, *San Martin*, was about 40 metres (131ft 3in) long, with a beam of about 10 metres (33ft). Such galleons carried guns on the main-deck in the waist, and down the length of the gun-deck below it, the bigger, heavier pieces being carried at this lower level. This led to the introduction of a marked tumble-home in the hull, the greatest width being at or just above the waterline, the beam reducing dramatically on the upper decks.

As well as incorporating the considerable advances in technology, later 16th and 17th century ships were marked by the increasingly ostentatious level of decoration they wore. *Sovereign of the Seas*, for example, had paint and gilt on every possible surface, and carving everywhere. The Swedish ship-of-the-line *Vasa* had a huge (two metres [6ft 6in] high by 3.25 metres [10ft 7in] wide) coat-of-arms – painted and gilded – across the entire width of her taffrail. The vessel boasted a total of over 700 individual carvings, and she was by no means an unusual example.

THE 100-GUN SHIP

By the 17th century, though marine infantrymen were still much in evidence, and close-order fighting skills were taught and used, there was a growing understanding that the capital warship was in essence a platform for guns. Ship-building technology had improved too, of course, and this inevitably meant that ships could grow in size to accommodate more and more guns of larger and larger calibres, so that by mid-century, the biggest ships were mounting up to 100 guns – and required a crew of almost 800 men.

By about 1660 sailing warships had staysails and jibs, as well as studding-sails flown outboard of the courses, and broadly speaking their sail-plans had grown enormously as the mechanics of handling sails and spars became better understood. There were more, and more efficient, mechanical aids, such as the windlass, and by about 1700, the steering wheel had appeared. From this point on virtually all warships had three masts.

Meanwhile, the European rush to colonise the world had been underway for some time, and had given rise to a new ship type that was faster, more lightly armed and more lightly manned than major warships. This type – the frigate – carried out the detailed work of surveying and mapping the globe and also provided protection for trading convoys and bases. The frigate was comparatively modest at first, being only half the length of a ship-of-the-line, and mounting perhaps two dozen of the smallest guns. Later, some frigates were built – for example, USS *Constitution* – that were vastly more heavily armed than that, and were serious competition for the smaller classes of ships-of-the-line, but these large frigates were almost an aberration.

THE MAN O' WAR AT ITS PEAK

Perhaps the most important feature of the frigates of the 18th century was the lowering of the after-castle by a deck, and the covering of the maindeck in the waist to form what is properly known as a spar deck. Thus, the ships had a single continuous deck from bow to stern, broken only by the short poop, which served as a command platform, a forerunner of the bridge. This style was eventually adopted for bigger vessels.

During the latter half of the 18th century, and on into the next, the wooden sailing warship reached the peak of its development, in vessels like Nelson's *Victory* and the Spanish flagship at Trafalgar, *Santissima Trinidad*. The three-decker first rate, with its 100 to 120 main guns, was virtually unsinkable, if properly handled, by any weapon then available. As a result, few ships were sunk in battle by gunfire, though many burned down to the waterline or were destroyed after taking so much punishment that they could no longer be manoeuvred. By the early 1820s, the shape of things to come had already been foreshadowed by the appearance of steam tugs to tow sailing warships in and out of harbour. Few would have believed, on the eve of Navarino, in October 1827, that two fleets of wooden sailing warships were about to meet in battle for the last time.

By the time of the Crimean War, less than three decades later, wooden men-o'-war were actually being towed into the firing line by steam tugs and proving very

ABOVE: *The frigate USS* Constitution *was launched in 1797. She remains in commission, berthed at Boston Navy Yard.*

vulnerable to the coastal batteries of new, improved guns. Significantly, the British and French had built armoured floating batteries, and three of the French ships made history by bombarding the Russian fortress at Kinburn in 1855. Though these craft were little more than barges covered in plate iron with crude steam engines giving them a top speed of barely two knots (they were towed to the Black Sea by paddle frigates), they gave the French the confidence to go ahead with an ironclad battleship, *Gloire*, which was launched in 1859. The British went one better the next year, with the bigger, all-iron *Warrior*.

Then, in 1862, the antagonists in the American Civil War put the mechanically powered armoured warship to the test at Hampton Roads, when the floating battery CSS *Virginia* (the former steam frigate USS *Merrimac*) fought an inconclusive action with the smaller turret ship USS *Monitor*. These two relied on steam power alone to get them about, but true seagoing ironclad steamers retained full sailing rig for some time yet because of the unreliability and heavy fuel consumption of early steam engines. The first seagoing battleship without masts and yards, HMS *Devastation*, was not launched until 1871.

The last third of the 19th century was a period of intense activity in naval design studios, laboratories, shipyards and armaments factories the world over. First, there was the race between arms and armour: new types of propellant gave new designs of shell more penetrating power; advances in metallurgy produced armour which was proof against new shells. Meanwhile, new types of boiler allowed new types of compound steam engine to operate at higher temperatures – and hence, higher pressure – and powerplants improved in leaps and bounds. Tactical and strategic requirements made their presence felt, too, and there were a number of experiments in weapons placement and mountings.

TURRET AND BARBETTE

The French favoured a 'lozenge' disposition of guns mounted on barbettes, platforms that rotated within a fixed armoured rampart. The Royal Navy, on the other hand, tended to favour guns mounted in turrets, enclosed armoured structures, the whole of which rotated. During the 1870s and early 1880s, the Royal Navy and certain others built a number of barbette ships to test the system, and a number of 'central battery' ships, with short box batteries to avoid the weight of a full-length armoured belt. After the Battle of Lissa in

1866, the leading navies also assumed that ramming tactics would be decisive, so designers reinforced the bow below the waterline in the hope of sinking an enemy by direct collision. Rams proved more dangerous to friends than foes, but the tactics also fostered a requirement for end-on firepower.

This resulted in a number of bizarre layouts – such as the en echelon (diagonal) arrangement seen in ships like the Italian *Andrea Doria* and the USS *Maine* – all of which worked better in theory than they did in practice.

MIXED-CALIBRE ARMAMENT

In the mid-1880s the revolving turret finally gave way to the compromise of a 'hooded barbette', the ancestor of the modern gun turret. After years of experiments and hybrid solutions the Royal Navy finally returned to the successful layout pioneered in *Devastation* – two twin mountings, one forward and one abaft a central superstructure containing the bridgework, light guns and boiler uptakes. This became the standard layout for battleships throughout the world until the turn of the century. The growing threat from torpedo boats, meanwhile, led to 'secondary' batteries of quick-firing guns, and by around 1900, most navies had adopted 'intermediate' batteries of guns up to 254mm (10in) calibre.

DREADNOUGHT

However, the splashes made as the different calibre shells landed complicated range-finding during battle, and the increased accuracy of main guns at long range further undermined the position of 'intermediate' batteries by extending the range at which battles could be fought. The revolutionary *Dreadnought* of 1906 went so far as to abandon all secondary guns except for light 76mm (3in) weapons. Other countries, notably Germany, retained medium-calibre (for example, 150mm [5.9in]) guns for their replies to *Dreadnought*, and within ten years every navy had followed suit – the threat from destroyers could not be ignored. The influence of *Dreadnought* had not been matched since the 1860s – henceforth all battleships copied the concept of a uniform armament of eight to 12 heavy-calibre guns, and the generic term 'dreadnought' was used to describe the new generation of large capital ships, such as Italy's Cavours and Germany's Nassaus.

THE BIG CRUISERS

The coming of steam engines and steel hulls had had an impact that was felt elsewhere in the fleet, beyond the capital ship. There was considerable confusion, for example, before an acceptable formula for a new type of cruising ship was finally reached. There was considerable variation in size, armament and armour of cruisers at this time. Indeed some – for example, Italy's Giuseppe Garibaldi class of armoured cruisers – were so big and powerful that debate raged over whether such vessels could operate in the line of battle, as well as in the traditional cruiser role. The carnage among armoured cruisers and the bigger battlecruisers (originally conceived as 'dreadnought' armoured cruisers) at Jutland proved the folly of placing these comparatively lightly armoured ships within the range of battleship guns.

There were potent developments down at the other end of the naval scale during that period, too, mainly thanks to Robert Whitehead, who pioneered the design of the locomotive torpedo in 1866. Whitehead gave the world a completely new type of weapon: one that travelled underwater, almost silently, under its own power, giving the boat which launched it time to clear the area before it hit its target or even if it missed. Whitehead's invention gave small boats the power to sink the biggest ships, and led to the development of modern torpedo boats (previously torpedo boats had been armed with the so-called spar torpedo, an explosive charge carried on the end of a long pole). Hard on the heels of the torpedo boats came the torpedo-boat destroyers – bigger craft, faster than the boats, and armed with more powerful quick-firing guns. Eventually these vessels grew and evolved into the destroyer.

Though locomotive torpedoes turned the small boat into a potent weapon, they soon found their true spiritual home to be the submarine. The story of submarine development is surprisingly brief. For centuries, man had tried to find a way to operate underwater, but technology had let him down. Now, in a period of not much over two decades, from 1879 to 1904, the engineering and materials available at last, the submarine became a viable proposition. Pioneers like John Holland wasted no time. His *Holland VI* was accepted by the United States Navy, and variants on his design went into service with many other fleets, including that of Britain. The Germans were latecomers to submarine warfare, but when they did finally embrace it, they went on to make the U-boat their most potent weapon in the Great War of 1914-1918. Boats like *U9*, which once sank three British cruisers in an hour, took a terrible toll of Allied shipping, and while they were finally defeated, they came close to winning the war.

THE WASHINGTON TREATY

The Great War never really came to a classic once-and-for-all sea battle. The conflict's principal naval engagement was the battle of Jutland, which really had no outright winner. Perhaps the war's most far-reaching maritime consequence was the 1922 Washington Naval Conference, which succeeded (if briefly) in limiting the size and number of the world's capital ships. Some existing ships, such as HMS *Queen Elizabeth*, the first of the 381mm (15in) gun battleships, were retained and re-fitted as necessary, but many others went for scrap. Some ships in the course of construction were re-planned, and subsequently became aircraft carriers, following the tentative but largely successful first steps towards establishing naval air forces that had been taken during World War I. Britain, America and Japan had led the way in converting large warships into carriers, but by the 1930s ships designed for the role had been built. *Enterprise* (CV6) wasn't the USN's first purpose-built carrier (that honour went to *Ranger*) but she was certainly the most distinguished of the new breed, taking part in almost all the US carrier battles in the Pacific during World War II.

THE BIG BATTLEWAGONS

With the demise of the naval treaties in the run-up to World War II, mighty battlewagons started to appear again – magnficent vessels, such as *Bismarck* and *Tirpitz*, *Scharnhorst* and *Gneisenau*, and *Yamato* and *Musashi* – the last-mentioned being the biggest battleships the world has ever seen. The Americans, too, built large battleships, and in *Iowa* and her three sister-ships, which entered service from 1943 onwards, procured an asset which was to be still in service almost 50 years later, having gone in and out of mothballs a number of times. Even so, as these mighty battlewagons were being commissioned, the carrier had arguably already superseded the battleship as the capital ship. Indeed carrier aircraft were to destroy both *Yamato* and *Musashi* and had already

BELOW: The open Trident missile launch tubes of the US nuclear-powered ballistic missile submarine Ohio. Ohio *undertook her first trials in June 1981 and her first operational deployment was in late 1982.*

had a hand in the sinking of *Bismarck*; *Tirpitz* also fell victim to aircraft, albeit land-based ones.

BEYOND THE CAPITAL SHIP

Further down the order of battle, meanwhile, cruisers had stabilised into two general types – those carrying eight-inch guns or thereabouts, and those armed with six-inch weapons. A fine example of the latter type was the Dutch cruiser *De Ruyter*, which went down fighting hopelessly superior Japanese forces at the battle of the Java Sea in February 1942.

Below this, destroyers, ships of anything up to 3,000 tonnes (2,950 tons) displacement, now provided fleet anti-submarine protection and served as convoy escorts, as well as taking on their enemy counterparts. The Allies between them operated vast numbers of destroyers on a wide range of duties, which even included, in the case of HMS *Cossack*, sending a boarding party onto a prison ship to release prisoners! Much smaller ships did sterling service, too – converted fishing trawlers and small corvettes in the Atlantic, motor torpedo boats, such as John F. Kennedy's *PT109*, with the USN in the Pacific.

World War II finally ended with the destruction of two Japanese cities with nuclear bombs, but in time nuclear energy was put to more creative use. Parsons' original 19th-century steam turbines had been used for two main purposes: to generate electricity for domestic use, and to power ships. Now nuclear energy was harnessed to produce steam to do these same jobs. In 1954, the USA launched its first nuclear-powered vessel, USS *Nautilus*, and she got 'Underway on nuclear power' on 17 January 1955. With hindsight, it is hardly surprising that she was a submarine, the first in a new class of vessel that was to change global strategic thinking profoundly.

THE NUCLEAR SUPERCARRIERS

Nuclear power as an energy source has much to recommend it to submarines: its production does not require oxygen and so a nuclear submarine can stay submerged – and hidden – for as long as its crew can stand the seclusion. It has a second advantage, too, that is applicable to ships in general: a cupful of nuclear fuel is enough to power a vessel for years. And for the other main class of nuclear-powered ships in use today – the aircraft carrier – the advantage of this is to free up all the space normally given over to fuel oil to the carriage of aviation fuel for its air group; it also allows the ship to stay on station for months at a time. The first of the nuclear carriers was *Enterprise* (CVN65), and she came complete with a nuclear-powered bodyguard, the guided-missile cruiser *Long Beach*. Since then, the Nimitz-class supercarriers have appeared, led by *Nimitz* herself, along with various classes of nuclear-powered cruiser, including the Russian *Kirov* and her sisters. Various types of nuclear-powered submarine are also now in service, among them ballistic missile submarines, such as the USS *Ohio* and her sister-boats (even though some submarines are over 25,000 tonnes [24,600 tons], they are still known as boats!).

MODERN DEVELOPMENTS

Conventional (non-nuclear) propulsion still has a very important role to play, but the long reign of the steam turbine is all but over for non-nuclear ships. Diesel engines now drive a wide range of ships in which speed is not a prime requirement. For destroyers, frigates and even light aircraft carriers, such as the Italian *Giuseppe Garibaldi* and similar-sized ships in the navies of Spain and Britain, the gas turbine is now widely favoured for its light weight, easy maintenance and rapid acceleration.

Conventionally powered submarines, like the Dutch Zeeleeuw class, are still driven, like their predecessors, by a combination of accumulator batteries and diesel generators, but strenuous efforts are being made to develop air-independent systems to extend underwater endurance. The Swedish Stirling closed cycle engine is now at sea, as is the German fuel cell system, and other navies are weighing up the advantages before selecting from a number of competing systems.

NEW MATERIALS

Steel is still the standard material for hull construction, but corrosion-resistant alloys are widely used for superstructures to keep weight down. Glass reinforced plastic (GRP) is widely used for specialised mine countermeasures vessels, and is coming into use to reduce radar reflections from superstructures.

Since its conception in the mists of time, the warship has always been at the forefront of technological development, and has always played a leading role in world events. Only the 'details' – propulsion methods and building materials, weapons, aids to observation and communication – have changed. The basic requirement remains the same, and the warship today is still no more nor less than a means of taking man upon the water so that he can fight there when he must.

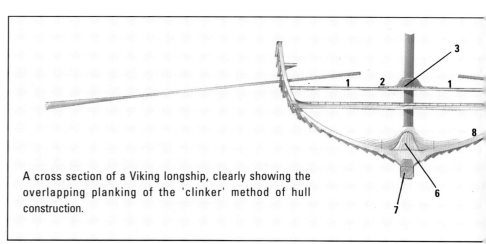

A cross section of a Viking longship, clearly showing the overlapping planking of the 'clinker' method of hull construction.

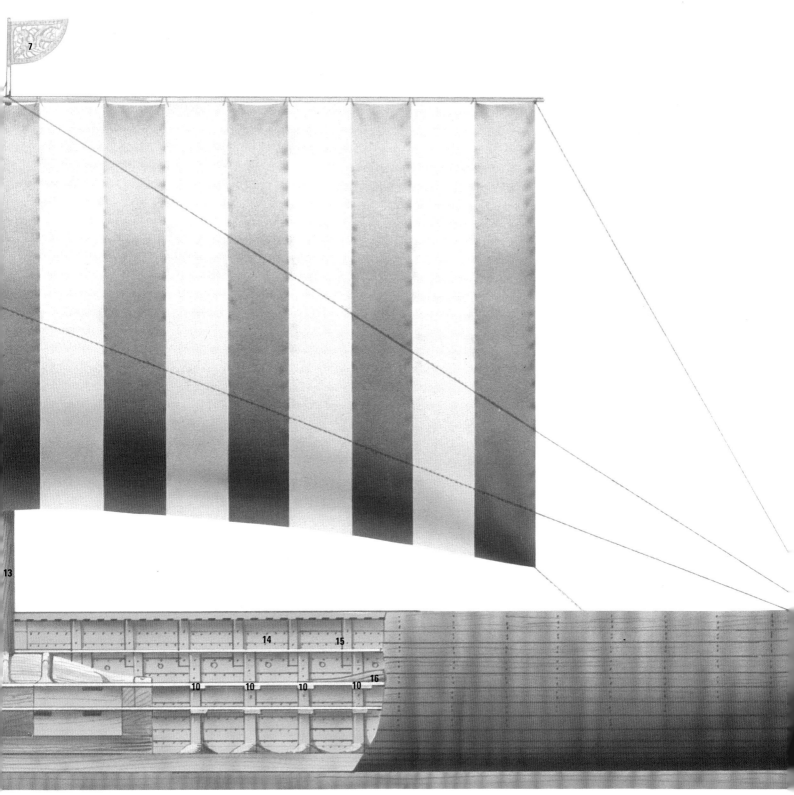

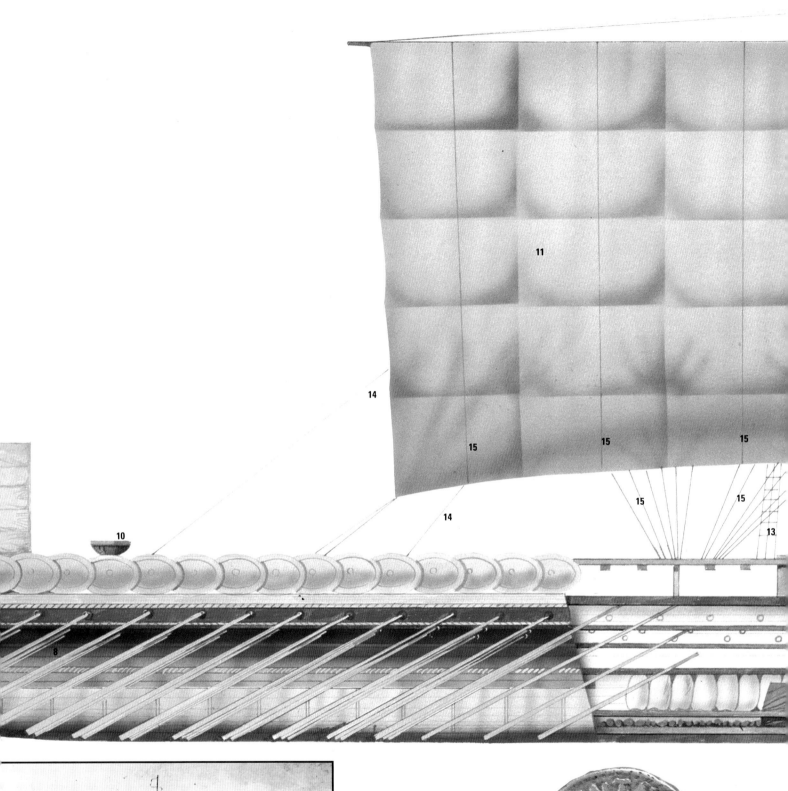

11

14

15 15 15

15 15

13

10

14

8

LEFT: This illustration showing a
Roman victory over the
Carthaginians in 256BC, during
the Punic Wars, depicts soldiers
boarding an enemy vessel across
the lowered corvus of a large
Roman trireme. RIGHT: A Roman coin
stamped with the image of a galley,
possibly a bireme, dating from 31BC, the year
of the historic battle of Actium in which Agrippa's smaller
craft outmanoeuvred the large warships of Mark Antony.

15   15   15   14   26

14   25   28

16   17   18   30

19   20   31

21   22   23   24

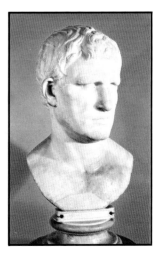

LEFT: This detail from an existing fragment of a mosaic relief, found in the Palazzo Barberini at Palestrina, depicts a Roman galley from approximately the first century BC. This type of bireme would probably have been built to protect merchant ships from marauding pirates, although they were also used as light warships alongside the larger triremes of the Roman fleet. RIGHT: A bust of Agrippa, Octavian's commander at sea, who routed Mark Antony's forces during the Battle of Actium.

LEFT: The restored Gokstad ship in the Viking Ship Museum, Oslo, Norway.
RIGHT: Ships figured in Norse mythology. Here the ship of Odin, chief among the Norse gods, transports those slain in battle to Valhalla. (From a runic stone from the island of Gotland.)
FAR LEFT: A carving on the Oseberg ship, a vessel used for the burial of a Norwegian princess in the 9th century.

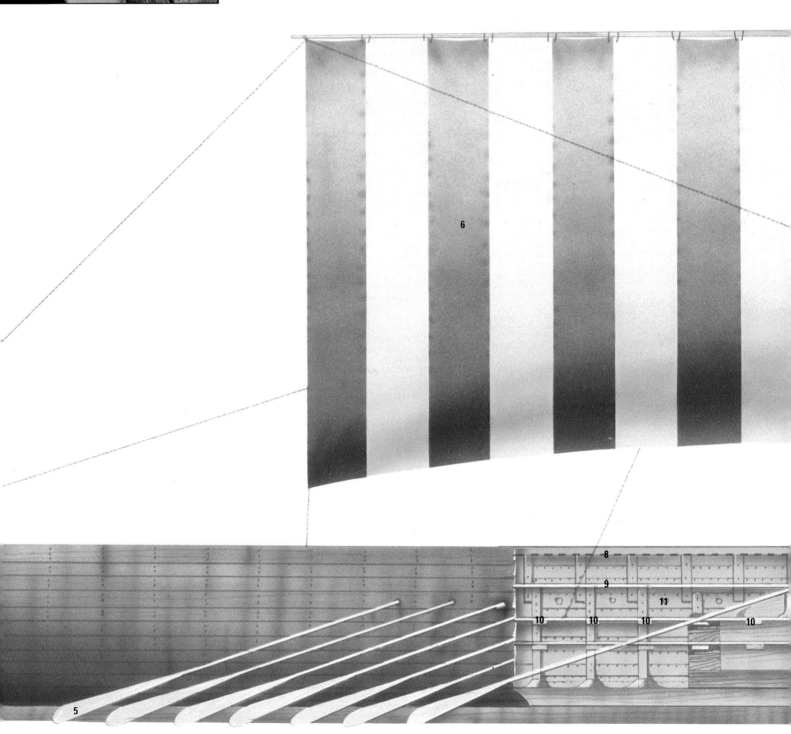

THE
VIKING
LONGSHIP

*T*he Vikings constructed a number of different types of ship to serve different purposes. Some were meant for trade alone, while some were dual-purpose vessels and were used for both trade and piracy. Longships were specialist war vessels used on pirate raids and in naval battles. They tended to be longer and slimmer in shape than the merchant vessels, and carried a large number of oars, whereas the traders were primarily sailing craft. The illustration shows a Viking longship of around AD 1000.

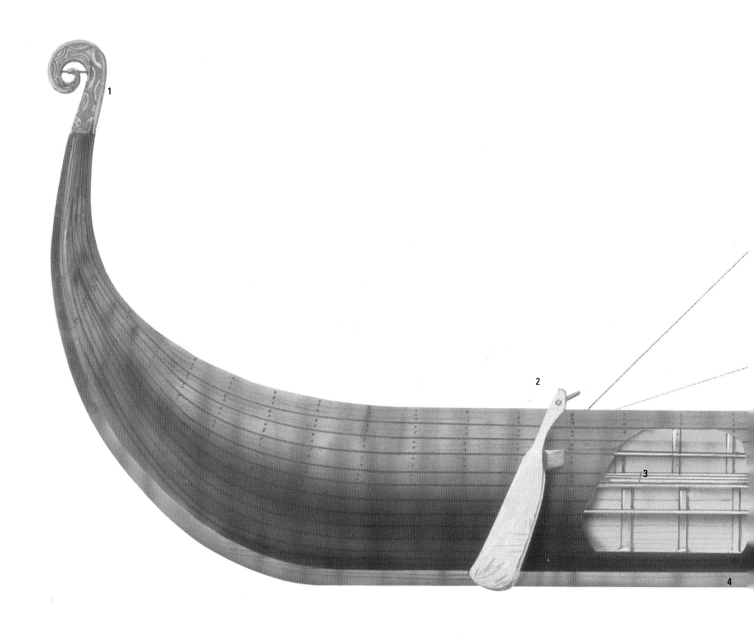

FLASH

- Mediterranean fighting galleys probably dated back to 3000BC – the last battle in which they fought was in 1717.

- A huge armoured ram was an integral part of the ship's prow, and almost certainly guaranteed the sinking of an adversary if good contact were made.

- Livy records that a squadron of triremes ran 203km (107 nautical miles) under sail across the Adriatic from Brundisium (Brindisi) to Corcyra (Corfu) in just 11 hours – an impressive average of almost 19km/h (10 knots).

- Galleys carried a mast and square sail for use when vessels were not in battle.

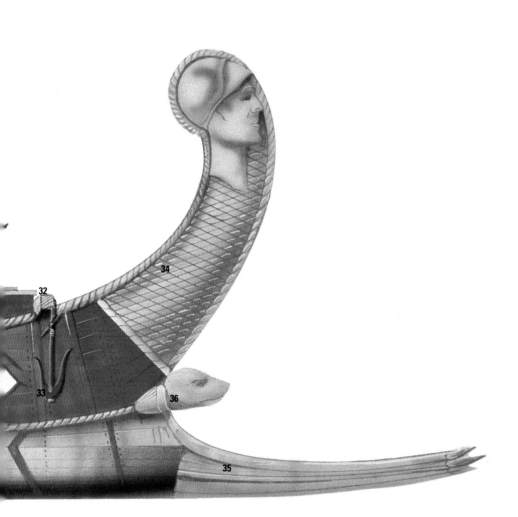

22. Keel	31. Rope for strengthening hull (to prevent warping)
23. Skids – usually hauled ashore at night	32. Cat head (anchor support)
24. Strengthening ribs	33. Anchor
25. Fighting platform	34. Prow
26. *Corvus* – used for troops boarding enemy ships	35. Ram (sheathed in bronze)
27. Spike – for locking ships together in battle	36. *Proembolion* (auxiliary ram) – to prevent damage to own hull when ramming
28. Support for *corvus*	
29. Catapult	
30. Strengthening blocks for ram	

THE
ROMAN
TRIREME

*T*he Roman trireme was bigger, heavier and more robust than its Greek counterpart and carried three banks of rowers. The oar holes on the lower tier would have been lined with leather sleeves to prevent seawater from entering the ship. Exact dimensions for such ships are unknown, but a typical Roman trireme would have been about 34 metres (112ft) long with a beam of approximately six metres (20ft), excluding outriggers, and a draught of one metre (3ft 3in). Traditionally, an 'eye' was painted on the bow to enable the trireme to 'see' her way across the seas.

1. Stern post
2. Bulwark
3. Shelter
4. Steering oar
5. Shields
6. Outrigger and top bank of oars
7. Middle bank
8. Lower bank
9. Oars of varying lengths for each level
10. Drum for beating time
11. Sail
12. Mast
13. Rope ladder
14. Steadying ropes for mast and spar
15. Ropes for folding sail
16. Platform for troops
17. Platform for oarsmen
18. Framing
19. Mast block
20. Water flasks/skins and food store
21. Ballast

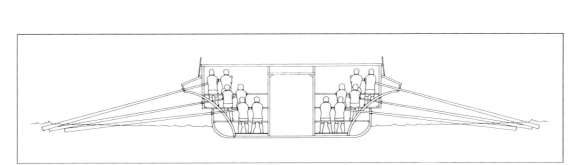

ABOVE: *A diagram showing one of the many theories put forward about the layout of oarsmen in a large Roman galley. Here there are two* **thranites** *whose oar passes through the outrigger; behind and slightly below them sit two* **zygites** *whose oar passes out through the hull; below and slightly behind them sit the* **thalamites***.*

FLASH

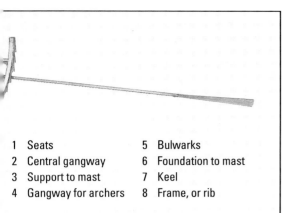

1	Seats	5	Bulwarks
2	Central gangway	6	Foundation to mast
3	Support to mast	7	Keel
4	Gangway for archers	8	Frame, or rib

CLINKER vs CARVEL

One thing all the Norse vessels had in common was their basic method of hull construction – the upper planks overlap the ones below them. This 'clinker' construction, which survived in large northern European ships until the 16th century, and is still seen in small boats today, was necessary because of a deficiency of simple technology. The northerners had not yet discovered the saw, and relied on the axe and the adze to cut and shape their timbers. Therefore, the relative precision required for edge-to-edge 'carvel' planking, as used in the Mediterranean, was unattainable. On the plus side, clinker construction allows the use of lighter framing, and needs less caulking to render it waterproof; on the minus side, it is much more difficult to join clinker planks together end to end, and this was one of the limitations on the size of the northern craft.

1. Stern post
2. Rudder
3. Spare oars
4. Keel
5. Oar
6. Sail (also used at night as cover for crew)
7. Weather vane
8. Spaces for hooking shields during combat
9. Platform for archers, etc (full length of ship)
10. Seats
11. Plugs/covers for oar apertures
12. Foundation for mast
13. Mast
14. Bulwarks
15. Framing of hull
16. Foundation block for auxiliary 'mast' (and to support sail when used as tent at night)
17. Stores (food, water flasks, arms and armour, shields, spare cordage, etc)
18. Anchor platform
19. Figurehead
20. Prow

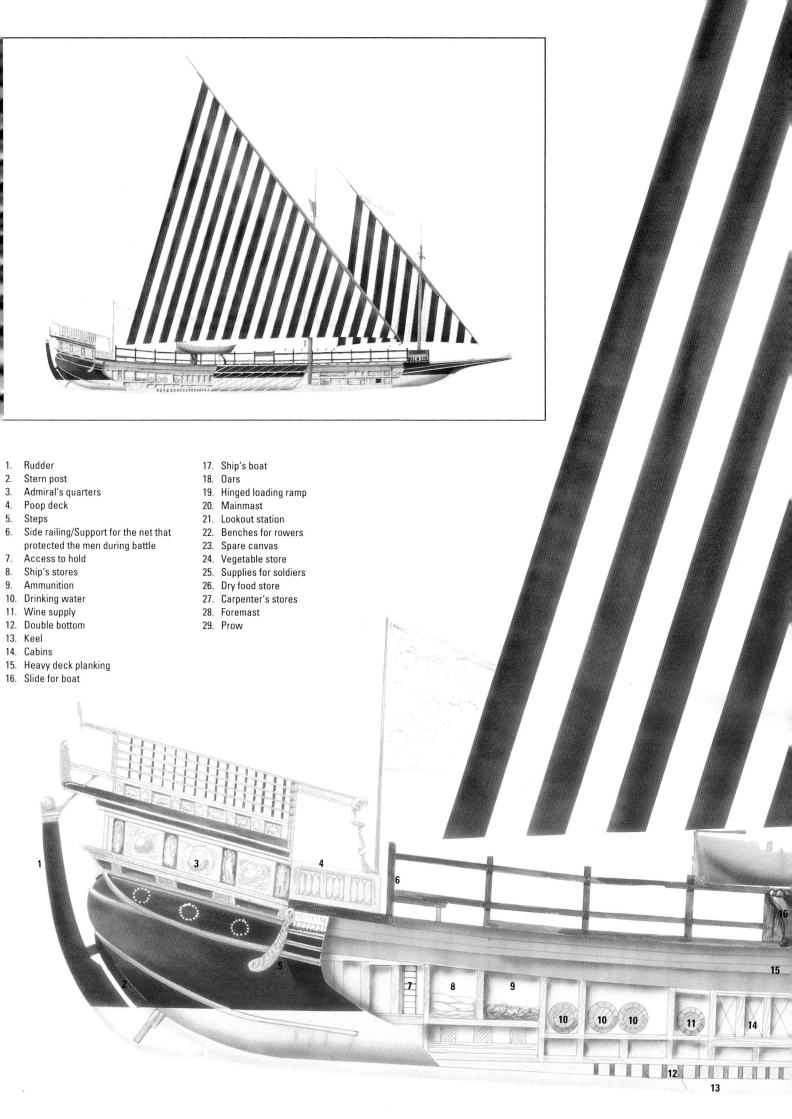

1. Rudder
2. Stern post
3. Admiral's quarters
4. Poop deck
5. Steps
6. Side railing/Support for the net that protected the men during battle
7. Access to hold
8. Ship's stores
9. Ammunition
10. Drinking water
11. Wine supply
12. Double bottom
13. Keel
14. Cabins
15. Heavy deck planking
16. Slide for boat
17. Ship's boat
18. Oars
19. Hinged loading ramp
20. Mainmast
21. Lookout station
22. Benches for rowers
23. Spare canvas
24. Vegetable store
25. Supplies for soldiers
26. Dry food store
27. Carpenter's stores
28. Foremast
29. Prow

THE
SPANISH
GALLEON

*W*hen the sailing warship took over from the oar-propelled galley as Spain's principal warship outside the Mediterranean, crews took some time to adjust to the new conditions. The ship's company consisted of soldiers, gunners and sailors, and the soldiers were in overall command, just as they had been on board the galleys. A Spanish galleon captain was in charge of the ship's navigation, but in all other respects answered to the military captain. The fighting tactic employed by the Spanish Navy at the time of the Armada still centred around boarding the enemy ship and overwhelming her crew in hand-to-hand fighting, and this strategy was reflected in the ship's complement which, for a ship of almost 1,000 tons, would have numbered about 150 seamen and gunners combined, plus 400 soldiers. The illustration shows San Martin, *the largest and most powerful of the royal galleons acquired by Philip II when he seized the throne of Portugal in 1580.*

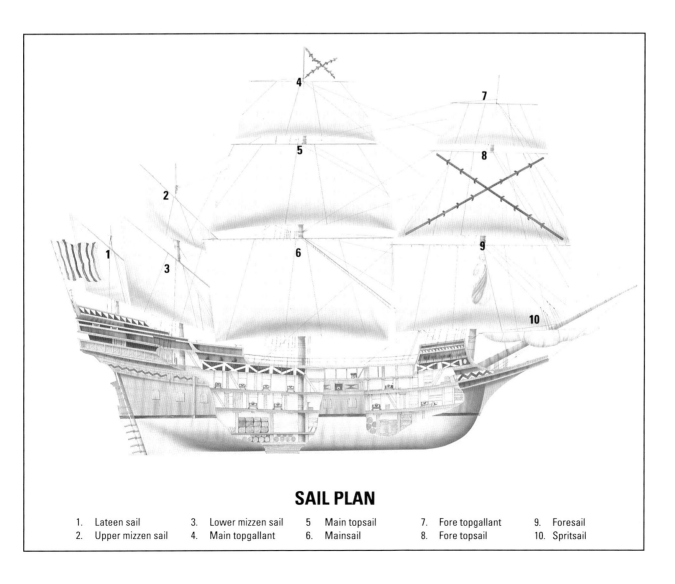

SAIL PLAN

1.	Lateen sail	3.	Lower mizzen sail	5.	Main topsail	7.	Fore topgallant	9.	Foresail
2.	Upper mizzen sail	4.	Main topgallant	6.	Mainsail	8.	Fore topsail	10.	Spritsail

FLASH

• Apart from the ordinary galleys that made up the bulk of the fleet, there were three categories of command galley. The largest and most ornate of these were the Royals, which were reserved for individuals of extremely exalted rank, such as captains-general of fleets. Next in size were the Capitanes, with 30-31 oars per side, and the third class were the Patrones, with 28-29 oars per side.

• With the arrival of the *scaloccio* system of rowing, with its single bank of oars each side, there was no longer any need to accommodate the oarsmen on different levels. The rowers for each oar sat on a single bench, though in some cases the team of five, six or even seven men may have been split into two groups. These sat facing each other, some pushing, while the others pulled. A significant result of this simplification of the rowing arrangements was an increase in the galley's top speed owing to a reduction in the craft's draught.

THE
ROYAL
GALLEY

*B*y the time of the Holy League's war against Turkish incursions into Europe, which culminated in the Battle of Lepanto in 1571, the war galley was reaching its peak of development. Yet, even after 2,000 years, its appearance had not changed very much from that of the ships the Ancient Greeks had used in classical times, except that experiments with different oar arrangements had demonstrated that one big oar was better than many smaller ones. In one respect, though, the galley in this period had become something different from its predecessors – it had become a gun platform, and thus was capable of damaging or destroying other craft from a distance.

ABOVE: Detail of the extraordinarily rich decoration along the outside of the galley's stern section.

ABOVE: A view aft into the vessel's sheltered poop, which housed the officers' quarters. This area was sumptuously decorated as befitted the flagship of the brother of King Philip II.

ABOVE: The galley was rowed by 420 oarsmen, sitting six men to each of the 35 oars per side. The oars were arranged on a single level.

FLASH

1. Stern light
2. Captain's gallery
3. Admiral's gallery
4. Tiller head
5. Rudder
6. Lateen mast
7. Mizzen mast
8. *Falconete* (breech-loading fixed musket)
9. Officers' quarters
10. Steering position
11. Companionway
12. *Pedrero* (smaller cannon)
13. Rubbing strip
14. Sickbay
15. *Culebrina* (larger cannon)
16. Bilge pump head
17. Bilge pump conduit
18. Flour store
19. Provisions
20. Sails
21. Ship's stores

22. Powder
23. Keel
24. Main mast
25. Upper walkway
26. Capstan
27. Anti-boarding nets
28. Anchor cable run to capstan
29. Crew's quarters
30. Shot locker
31. Bowsprit foundation
32. Gunport
33. Master-at-Arms and troops' quarters
34. Lamp room
35. Fresh water
36. Cordage
37. Anchor cable
38. Foremast
39. Bowsprit
40. Beak
41. Prow

• A three-masted ship with square sails on the fore and main masts, a lateen sail on the mizzen and a spritsail on the bowsprit, *San Martin* was 37.3 metres (122ft 3in) long, 9.3 metres (30ft 5in) abeam and displaced around 1,000 tons. Under the command of the Duke of Medina Sidonia, she became the flagship of Spain's Invincible Armada against the English in 1588, and was one of the 67 ships out of a fleet of 130 that safely returned to Spain after the conflict.

• Conditions aboard the galleons of the Armada fleet were appalling; the sailors were considered the least important element in the chain of command and their pay was very much in arrears. Accordingly, many seamen actually died from hunger. On the epic voyage home to Spain after the conflict it is said that in the region of 10,000 men died, and although many of them were victims of shipwreck during storms, many more deaths were caused by sickness, starvation and thirst aboard ship.

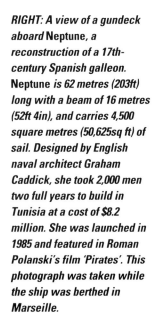

RIGHT: A view of a gundeck aboard Neptune, *a reconstruction of a 17th-century Spanish galleon.* Neptune *is 62 metres (203ft) long with a beam of 16 metres (52ft 4in), and carries 4,500 square metres (50,625sq ft) of sail. Designed by English naval architect Graham Caddick, she took 2,000 men two full years to build in Tunisia at a cost of $8.2 million. She was launched in 1985 and featured in Roman Polanski's film 'Pirates'. This photograph was taken while the ship was berthed in Marseille.*

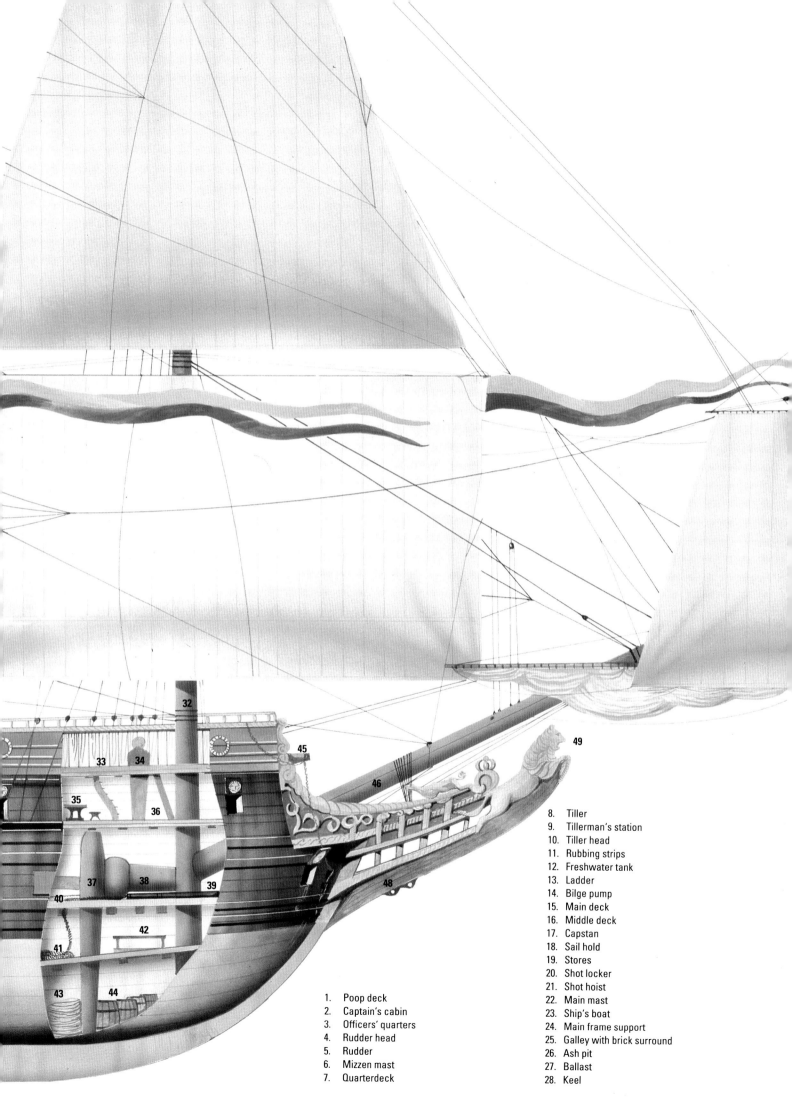

8. Tiller
9. Tillerman's station
10. Tiller head
11. Rubbing strips
12. Freshwater tank
13. Ladder
14. Bilge pump
15. Main deck
16. Middle deck
17. Capstan
18. Sail hold
19. Stores
20. Shot locker
21. Shot hoist
22. Main mast
23. Ship's boat
24. Main frame support
25. Galley with brick surround
26. Ash pit
27. Ballast
28. Keel

1. Poop deck
2. Captain's cabin
3. Officers' quarters
4. Rudder head
5. Rudder
6. Mizzen mast
7. Quarterdeck

SOVEREIGN
OF THE SEAS

*T*he Sovereign of the Seas *was a vessel of great influence on future shipbuilding and on naval warfare as a whole. Although she was quite cumbersome, and was refitted twice, she represented two important trends. The first was the English Naval Board's insistence on the maximum weight of firepower; this also meant that she had to be relatively low in the water compared with 16th-century ships as the recoil from her fearsome broadside would not permit high forecastles or aftcastles. Secondly, her sails set the design for the future, in the number of masts and the sail plan. But in one sense, she was a return to the past: her gorgeous decoration was not at all functional, and represented mere vain glory on the part of the monarch Charles I.*

ABOVE: The second battle of the Texel, fought on 11 August 1673, in which the Royal Sovereign, as she was by then known, served as Prince Rupert's flagship. RIGHT: The sail plan. The Sovereign of the Seas carried sails on her three masts and on the bowsprit. The main and foremast were each rigged with four sails – mainsail, topsail, topgallant and royal; the mizzenmast carried a lateen sail and two square-rigged sails; and the bowsprit carried two sails.

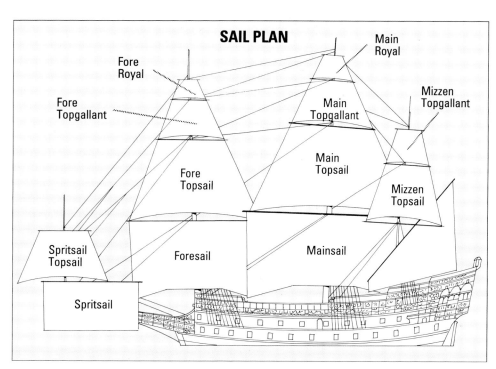

SAIL PLAN

Fore Royal

Main Royal

Fore Topgallant

Main Topgallant

Mizzen Topgallant

Fore Topsail

Main Topsail

Mizzen Topsail

Spritsail Topsail

Foresail

Mainsail

Spritsail

FLASH

• One thousand oak trees were used in the *Vasa*'s construction. This seems an enormous number for a ship that displaced 1,150 tons. However, contemporary accounts of other Royal Ships tell a similar story. *Prince Royal*, a vessel of around 1,033 tons built in England by Phineas Pett in 1608, used approximately 1,627 trees. Just to obtain so much timber was difficult, and the Swedes, for their part, had declared the oak tree a protected species long before the *Vasa* was built.

• *Vasa* originally had 64 cannon, of which only three now remain; 53 of the others were sold to Germany after they were salvaged in 1664. The 48 x 24-pounders each weighed around 1.5 tonnes and had a crew of seven. A good rate of fire would have been 10 shots per hour.

• The Swedish Navy did not have hammocks until 1676, and so the crew of the *Vasa,* had her career not been tragically cut short, would have slept on the decks by the guns.

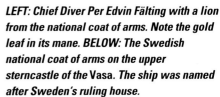

LEFT: Chief Diver Per Edvin Fälting with a lion from the national coat of arms. Note the gold leaf in its mane. BELOW: The Swedish national coat of arms on the upper sterncastle of the Vasa. *The ship was named after Sweden's ruling house.*

9. Bread store
0. Lower deck
1. Serving area for galley
2. Foremast
3. Foredeck
4. Stanchion
5. Crew's quarters
6. Carpenter's area
7. Bowsprit foundation
8. Bowsprit support
9. Hawsepipe to anchor cable
0. Anchor cable
1. Cable store
2. Surgeon's area
3. Cordage
4. Powder magazine
5. Cathead
6. Bowsprit
7. Anchor port
8. Prow
9. Figurehead

VASA

*A*s a Royal Ship, Vasa *was designed to impress, and indeed her hull decoration was, and is, stunning. Hundreds of gilded and painted figures adorn her upper works, and the entire taffrail above the upper of the two stern galleries is occupied by a huge representation of the coat of arms of the house of Vasa. This carving alone, executed personally by Martin Redtmer, the supervising woodcarver on the ship, is 2 metres (6ft 5in) high and 3.25 metres (10ft 6in) wide. In all, there were over 700 individual carvings decorating the ship.*

SAIL PLAN

1. Mizzen topsail
2. Mizzen
3. Main topgallant
4. Main topsail
5. Main
6. Fore topgallant
7. Fore topsail
8. Fore
9. Spritsail topsail
10. Spritsail

GREAT MEN OF THE SEA

PHINEAS AND PETER PETT

The Petts were a dynasty of shipwrights. Phineas himself was the son of a master shipwright who died in 1592. Appointed keeper of the plank yard at Chatham dockyard, the first vessel the young Pett designed and built was launched in 1604. He was then, at the surprisingly young age of 35, appointed master shipwright. His first large commission was to build the *Prince Royal*. This vessel was the largest then built in England, but Pett made several mistakes such as underestimating the amount of timber required and using unseasoned wood.

In spite of these flaws, the *Prince Royal* marked a determination on the part of the English to build large vessels, and the *Sovereign of the Seas* 25 years later was the culmination of this process. For this latter vessel, Pett had learnt from his experiences, and there were none of the problems he had encountered before.

Pett's great strength was his ability to get on with the monarchs he served (James I and Charles I), and this diplomatic skill stood him in good stead on several occasions: a commission of 1608, for example, found that he had built a 160-ton ship privately, but using dockyard timber. On this occasion, as on many others, however, he was merely reprimanded.

In 1647, Phineas was succeeded by his son Peter (shown above with the *Sovereign*) as commissioner of Chatham dockyard. This son refitted the *Sovereign* as a two-decker. Although a very able shipwright, he was an unpopular character, who was as corrupt as his father, and he was disgraced after the Dutch raid on the Medway dockyards in 1667.

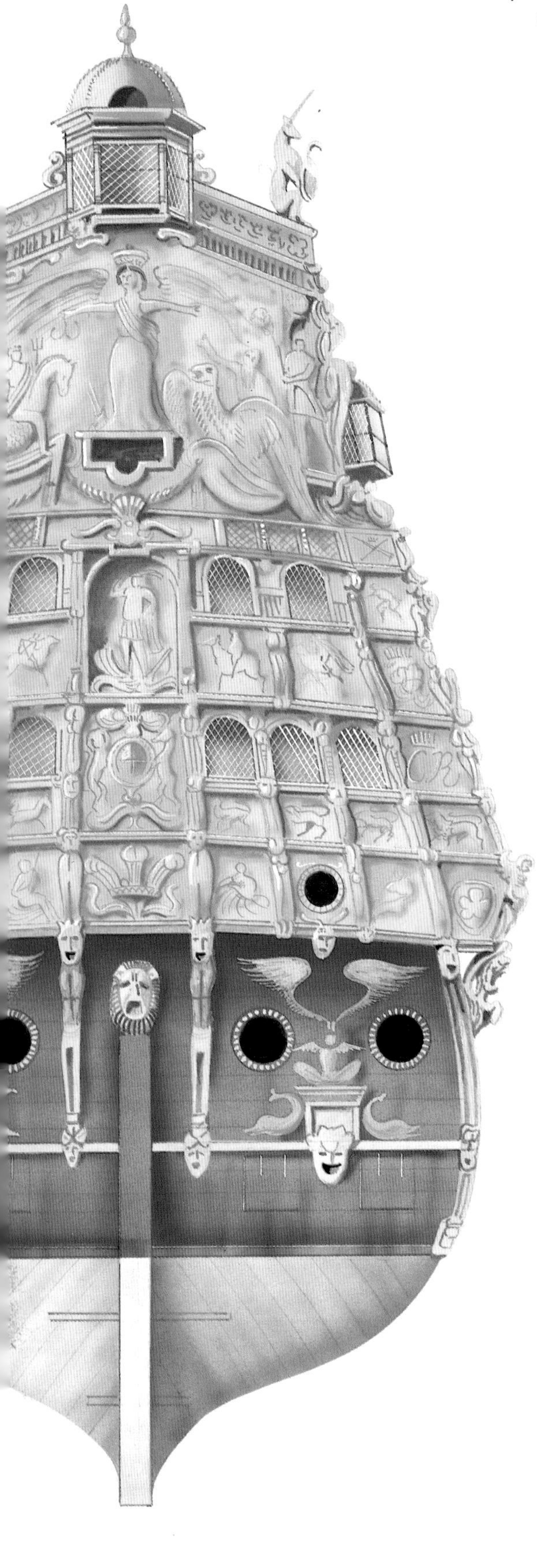

Sails
1. Spritsail
2. Spritsail topsail
3. Foresail
4. Fore topsail
5. Mainsail
6. Main topsail
7. Mizzen
8. Mizzen topsail

Masts
9. Bowsprit
10. Foremast
11. Mainmast
12. Mizzenmast
13. Spritsail topmast

Rigging
14. Forestay
15. Fore topmast stay
16. Fore topgallant stay
17. Mainstay
18. Main topgallant stay
19. Mizzen stay
20. Mizzen topgallant stay
21. Mizzen lift
22. Martnets
23. Bowline
24. Fairleads

Hull
25. Figurehead
26. Keel
27. Forecastle
28. Forecastle for halyards etc
29. Upper deck
30. Quarter deck
31. Poop deck
32. Officers' cabin
33. Captain's cabin/State room
34. Storage for flags
35. Navigator's cabin
36. Ward room
37. Closed gallery
38. Galley area
39. Fore galley area
40. Upper gun deck
41. Main gun deck
42. Lower gun deck
43. Riding bits for anchor cables
44. Stairs
45. Deck supports
46. Main pump
47. Orlop deck (used as hospital in action)
48. Stores
49. Capstan
50. Rubbing strips
51. Entry port
52. Rudder
53. Stove
54. Anchor
55. Whipstaff (controlling rudder)

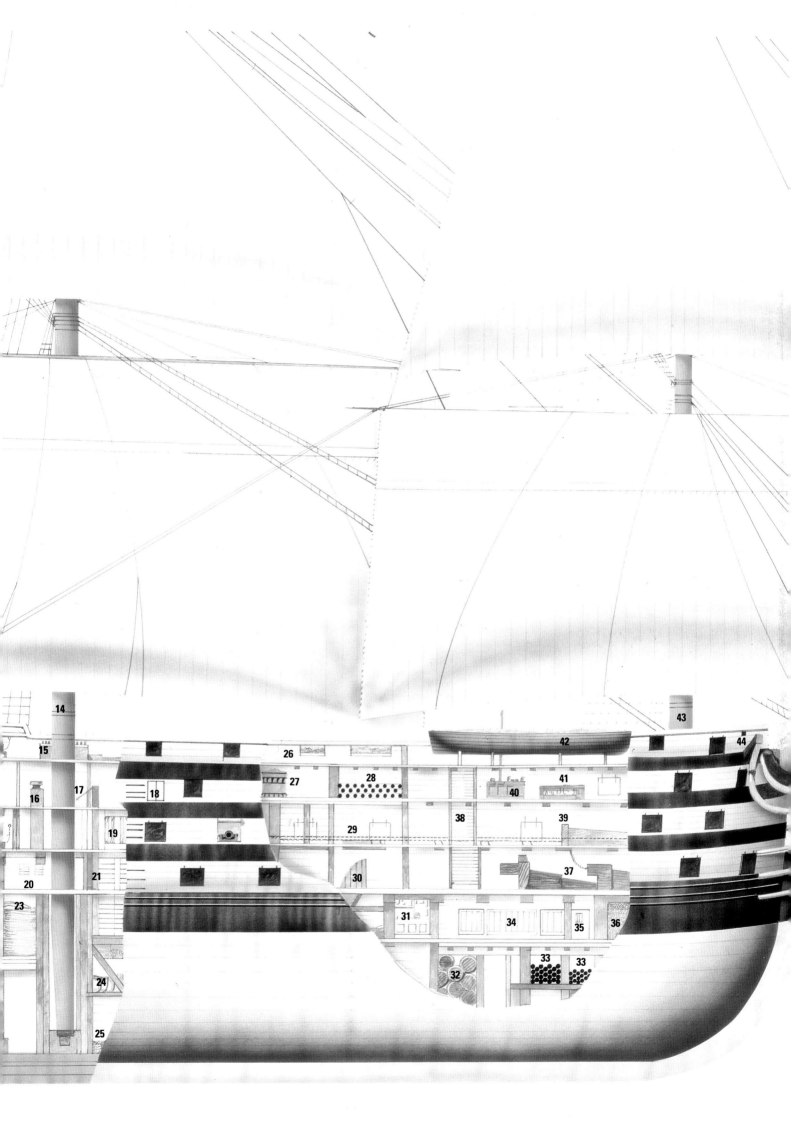

ixed ladder
ntry port
ubbing strip
heathing
eel
nchor
ipe to stove
Muster area for marines
orecastle (crew accommodation)

45. Main capstan
46. Stove/Galley
47. Officers' wardroom/sleeping quarters (midshipmen etc)
48. Lower deck
49. Chain lead to anchor
50. Cleaning area for cable
51. Mooring bitts
52. Fore storage area (sometimes

used for livestock)
53. Fore powder room
54. Hanging magazines for stowage of ready-made ammunition
55. Stowage lockers
56. Forward shot area
57. Forward magazine
58. Sail locker
59. Cable locker

60. Main magazine
61. Bilge
62. Inner planking/Framing
63. Foremast
64. Shrouds
65. Cathead
66. Bitt for tensing bowsprit
67. Bowsprit
68. Prow

RIGHT: **HMS Victory** *today, restored to her original glory, in special dry dock at Portsmouth dockyard. After the Napoleonic Wars* **Victory** *was due to be scrapped, but there was public outcry and she became a stationary flagship for the Commander-in-Chief at Portsmouth. Princess Victoria – later Queen Victoria – visited here there, awakening further interest in the ship. In 1922 the 'Save the* **Victory** *Fund' was set up to fully restore her and open her to the public as an historic monument.*

1. Captain's cabin
2. Captain's study
3. Steering wheel
4. Admiral's cabin
5. Plotting room
6. Officers' cabins
7. Water tanks
8. Admiral's staff
9. Wardroom
10. Officers' stores
11. Rudder
12. Poop deck
13. Mizzen mast
14. Main mast
15. Belaying pins
16. Stanchion for securing heavy weights below deck
17. Pump
18. Entry port
19. Hammock storage
20. Lamp room
21. Pipe to bilge
22. Sail room
23. Cordage room
24. Bread/Biscuit storage
25. Ballast
26. Netting rack
27. Capstan
28. Ready ammunition rack
29. Anchor chain
30. Entry cover
31. Sick bay
32. Powder magazine
33. Shot magazine
34. Small arms lockers
35. Prison
36. Chain locker
37. Main and auxiliary entry ports to chain locker
38. Companionway
39. Hawespipe entry
40. Galley
41. Sailmakers'/Carpenters' working area
42. Ship's boat
43. Fore mast
44. Cathead
45. Bow sprit
46. Figurehead

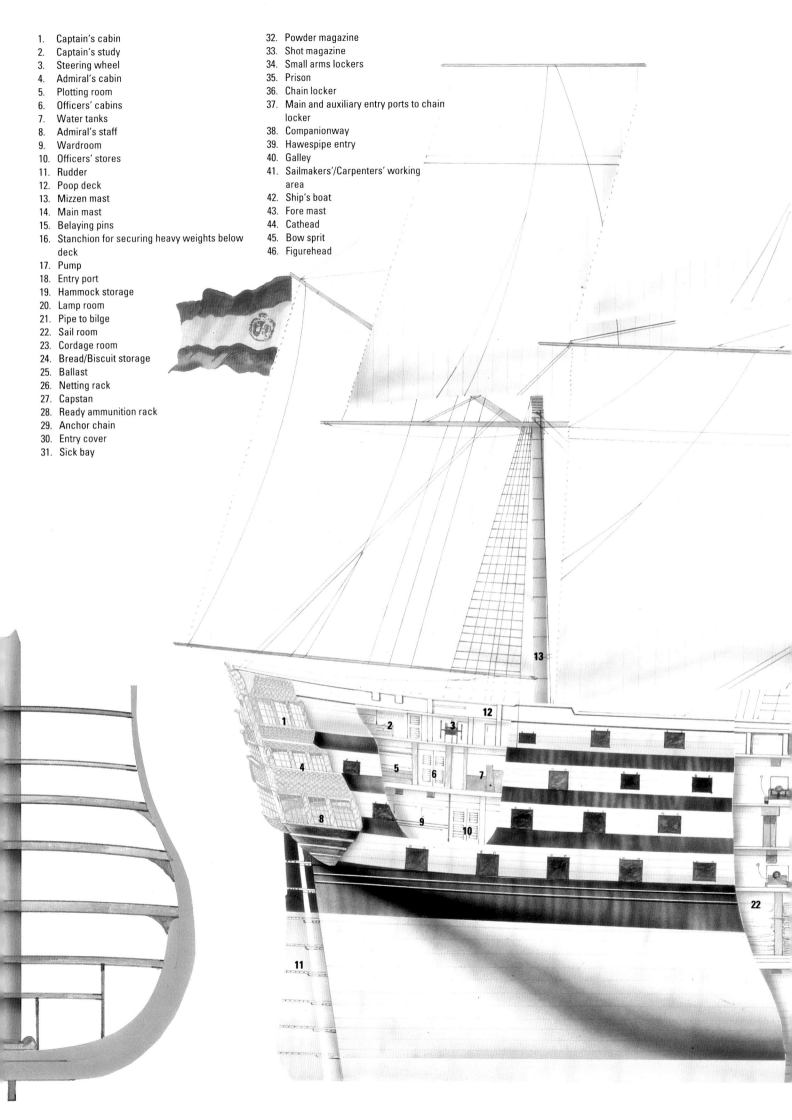

SANTISSIMA TRINIDAD

A s originally built at the Arsenal of Havana, Cuba, in 1769, the mighty Santissima Trinidad *was a three-decker constructed along the lines of the three-decker warships then in favour in England. By the time she met the British fleet at the Battle of Trafalgar in 1805, she had been converted to a four-decker mounting 136 guns. This made her the biggest ship in the world at the time, and it is likely that her poor performance, and ultimate loss, during the historic battle was due to her being overloaded with ordnance.*

BELOW: This section throu■ Santissima Trinidad's ster■ shows her pronounced tun■ home and massive framing■ broadness lower down wa■ essential for stability due ■ increased height of a fourt■

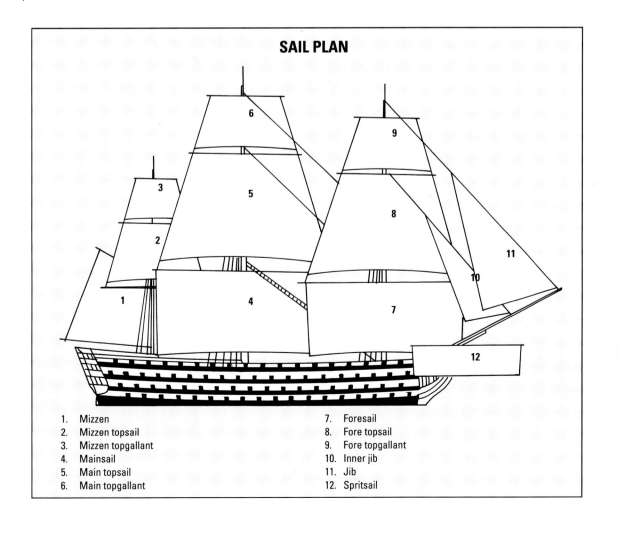

SAIL PLAN

1.	Mizzen	7.	Foresail
2.	Mizzen topsail	8.	Fore topsail
3.	Mizzen topgallant	9.	Fore topgallant
4.	Mainsail	10.	Inner jib
5.	Main topsail	11.	Jib
6.	Main topgallant	12.	Spritsail

GREAT MEN OF THE SEA

SIR THOMAS MASTERMAN HARDY 1769-1839

Captain Sir Thomas Masterman Hardy's first command was a prize brig, the *Mutine*, which he captured while serving under Admiral Lord Nelson at Santa Cruz some months before the Battle of the Nile (1 August 1798). After the

battle Hardy transferred to Nelson's flagship *Vanguard* as flag captain. After this time Nelson and Hardy were rarely separated. He joined Nelson on *Victory* in 1803 for the blockade of Toulon, and was again at Nelson's side at the Battle of Trafalgar (he was created a baronet for his part in that action). In 1825 he became a rear admiral, and five years later was promoted to First Sea Lord of the Admiralty, a post he held until 1834. Sir Thomas died in 1839 in his seventieth year.

***ABOVE:** The anchor winch on* Victory *'s lower gun deck.*

***RIGHT:** Nelson's cabin, and officers' dining area, aboard* Victory. *Accommodation for senior officers was luxurious compared to the conditions in which the crew had to live. However, sanitation was poor for officers and men alike, there being no facilities for bathing. Only salt water was available for washing both clothes and body.*

VICTORY

Victory was a First Rate line-of-battle ship, which meant that she carried at least 100 guns, spread over three main gun decks. Her armament changed a number of times during her long career, but for her most famous battle – Trafalgar, on 21 October 1805 – she carried thirty 32-pounders on the lower deck, twenty-eight 24-pounders on the middle deck, thirty 12-pounders on the upper deck, ten 12-pounders on the quarterdeck, and two 68-pound carronades on the forecastle. The last were the biggest in service with the Royal Navy and had tremendous destructive power at close range. The illustration shows Victory *as she was before the battle.*

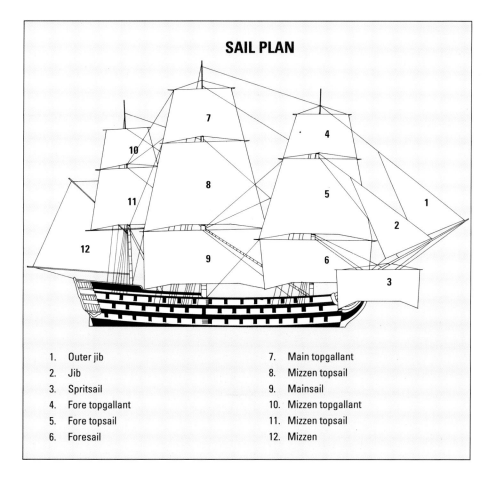

SAIL PLAN

1. Outer jib	7. Main topgallant
2. Jib	8. Mizzen topsail
3. Spritsail	9. Mainsail
4. Fore topgallant	10. Mizzen topgallant
5. Fore topsail	11. Mizzen topsail
6. Foresail	12. Mizzen

FLASH

• Although a very large ship, by the standards of the day *Santissima Trinidad* was not a particularly big ship for the number of cannon she carried, being 61.2 metres (200ft) long and 19.2 metres (62ft 9in) wide. As she appeared at the Battle of Trafalgar, *Santissima Trinidad* carried 130 guns compared to *Victory*'s 100.

• In her final four-deck form, *Santissima Trinidad* carried 32 x 36-pounders on her lower deck, 16 to a side. On her upper deck she had 34 x 24-pounders, and on her top two decks she carried 36 x 12-pounders, 18 x eight-pounders and 10 x 24-pound howitzers (which were much shorter than cannon). In the unlikely event of all the guns on one side firing together, the ship would have delivered 665kg (302lb) of iron shot at a time, if all were single-shotted. In fact, at close range, guns were often double- or even triple-shotted whenever time allowed.

• In contrast, *Victory* mounted 30 x 32-pounders, 28 x 24-pounders, 40 x 12-pounders and two 68-pound carronades for a maximum broadside delivery of 522kg (236lb) of iron shot at a time.

45

46

RIGHT: This painting of the Battle of Trafalgar by F. Sartorius (c.1775-c.1830) depicts the moment of Santissima Trinidad's dismasting by two broadsides from HMS Neptune just before 14.30 on 21 October 1805. The ships shown are, from left to right: Victory, Redoubtable, Téméraire, Fougueux, Santissima Trinidad, Neptune, Bucentaur, Conqueror, Royal Sovereign and Santa Ana.

ABOVE: The first clash between ironclads: Hampton Roads, 9 March 1862.

ABOVE : Rear Admiral John A. Dahlgren (centre), w
commander in the US Navy developed the gun that
name. Merrimack carried 228mm (9in) Dahlgrens w
fire shell or solid shot. Dahlgrens were introduced
Navy in 1859, and their shape – very thick at the bre
with a narrow muzzle end – led to them becoming k
'ginger beer bottles'. At the outbreak of the Civil Wa
was in command of Washington Navy Yard; the pic
him as commander of the South Atlantic Blockadin
to which post he was appointed in 1863.

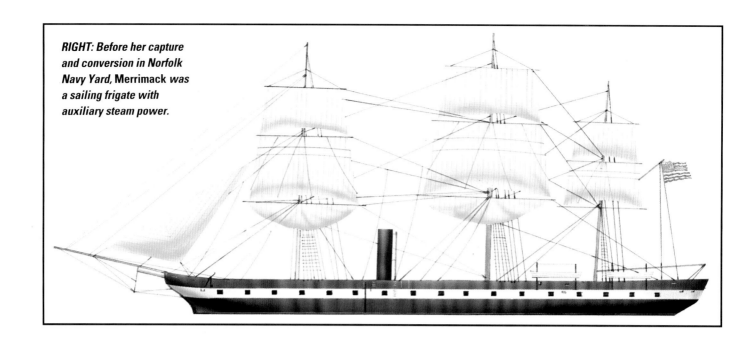

RIGHT: Before her capture and conversion in Norfolk Navy Yard, Merrimack *was a sailing frigate with auxiliary steam power.*

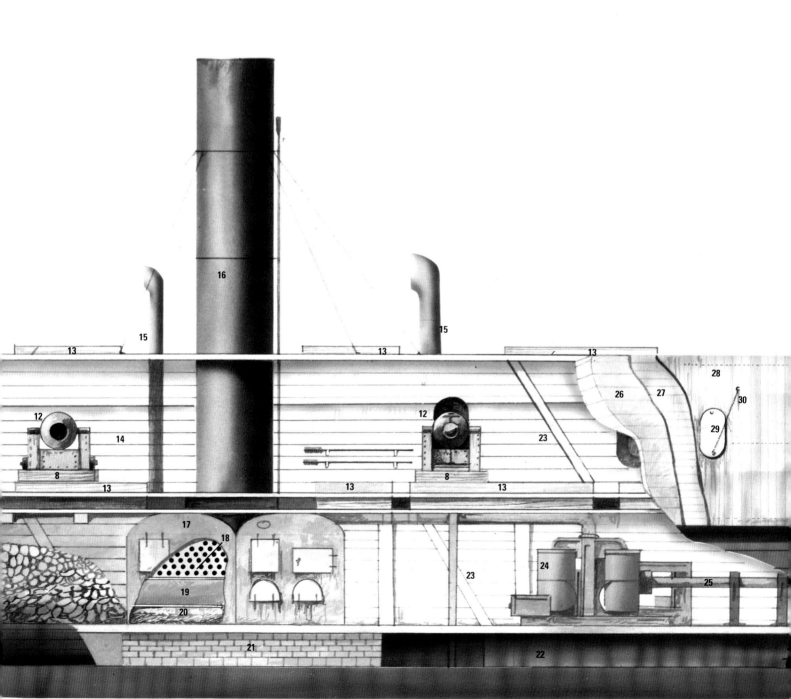

MERRIMACK

*A*lthough almost always referred to by her Union name of Merrimack, *this ship had been renamed CSS* Virginia *by the time she took part in the action at Hampton Roads that was to make her famous. The main illustration shows her as she would have looked on the morning of 8 March 1862, before she set off to engage the Union blockading force. By the time she fought* Monitor, *the following day, her ram had been lost, her funnel and ventilators had been badly damaged and she had also received considerable damage to her superstructure.*

1. Ram
2. False bow
3. Cathead
4. Anchor
5. Keel
6. Pilot house
7. 178mm (7in) rifled gun
8. Timber mount
9. Confederate jack
10. Stove
11. Coal bunker (anthracite)
12. 228mm (9in) rifled Dahlgren gun
13. Hatch combing with grating
14. Crew area (crew were mostly kept ashore because of poor conditions; if serving aboard, then the gun deck was used for sleeping etc)
15. Ventilator
16. Funnel
17. Martin tubular boiler
18. Tubes for producing steam
19. Grate
20. Ash pit
21. Brick foundation to boilers
22. Bilge
23. Companion way
24. Horizontal back-acting engines with 914mm (36in) stroke
25. Shaft

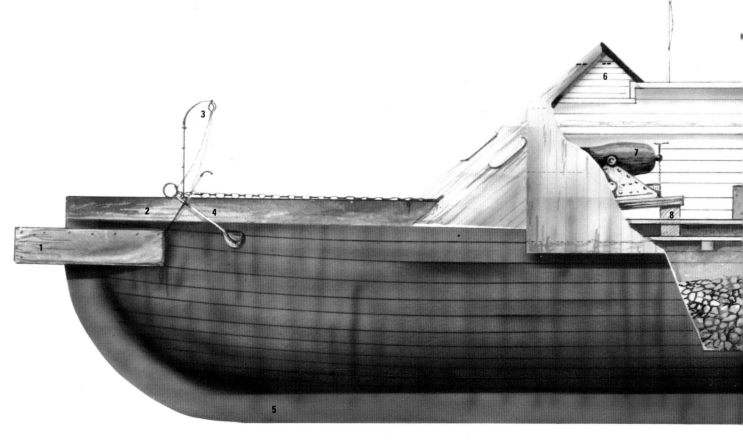

FLASH

• The hull of USS *Constitution* was constructed from oak from Massachusetts, Maine and Georgia, and was braced to withstand abnormal stresses. The bolts used to hold its timbers in place and the copper sheathing for the hull's bottom were manufactured by Paul Revere, a Boston silversmith and nationalist, whose 'midnight ride' to warn of the approach of British troops at the start of the American Revolutionary War was made famous by the Longfellow poem. *Constitution*'s masts were of white pine, and the total cost of the ship was around $302,000.

• *Constitution*'s original figurehead was a carving of Hercules brandishing a club. In 1807 this was changed to one of Neptune, while in the War of 1812 the ship carried a decorative 'billet head' but no figurehead. In the 1830s a portrait of President Jackson was installed. This caused considerable acrimony, and despite a guard being mounted the head was cut off and stolen. It was later found and re-installed. Today *Constitution* has no figurehead.

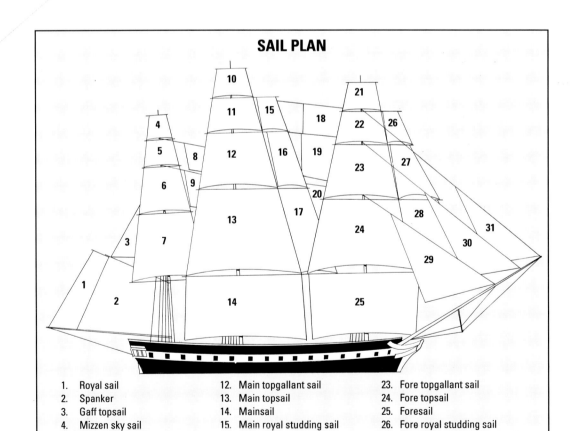

SAIL PLAN

1. Royal sail
2. Spanker
3. Gaff topsail
4. Mizzen sky sail
5. Mizzen royal
6. Mizzen topgallant sail
7. Mizzen topsail
8. Mizzen royal staysail
9. Mizzen topgallant staysail
10. Main sky sail
11. Main royal

12. Main topgallant sail
13. Main topsail
14. Mainsail
15. Main royal studding sail
16. Main topgallant studding sail
17. Main top studding sail
18. Main royal staysail
19. Main topgallant staysail
20. Main top staysail
21. Fore sky sail
22. Fore royal

23. Fore topgallant sail
24. Fore topsail
25. Foresail
26. Fore royal studding sail
27. Fore topgallant studding sail
28. Fore top studding sail
29. Fore topmast staysail
30. Jib
31. Outer jib

CONSTITUTION

The design of the first generation of US Navy vessels was entrusted to Joshua Humphreys, a prominent Philadelphia shipwright, and his plans, developed with the aid of William Doughty and an Englishman, Josiah Fox, culminated in the construction of the biggest, most powerful frigates afloat. The first ship, one of the three 44s, was called appropriately USS United States *and was launched at Philadelphia on 10 May 1797; the second ship, one of the three 36/38s, was christened USS* Constellation *and slipped into the water at Baltimore on 7 September; the third ship was* Constitution *herself, and she slipped down the ways six weeks later. Her builders could little have dreamed that she would still be in commission 100 years later and proudly on display in her native city.*

1. Mizzen mast
2. Steering position
3. Captain's quarters
4. Wardroom
5. Officers' quarters
6. Tiller room
7. Tiller
8. Lamp room
9. Stern fresh water tank
10. Canvas
11. Rudder
12. Cordage
13. Magazine
14. Ship's boat
15. 32-pounder carronades
16. Capstan
17. Main mast
18. Stairway
19. 24-pounder 'long' gun
20. Bilge pump
21. Fresh water pump
22. Ship's access ladder
23. Ship's stores

24. Pipes to bilge pump
25. Pipe to fresh water pump
26. Ship's provisions
27. Sick bay
28. Shot room
29. Bilge
30. Main fresh water tank
31. Fore mast
32. Anti-boarding netting (stowed)
33. Cathead
34. Galley
35. Bowsprit support
36. Ship's carpenter
37. Diagonal bracing beams
38. Anchor cable well
39. Powder filling room
40. Forefoot
41. Anchor cable ports
42. Bowsprit

TOP: The brig of the USS Constitution. *ABOVE: USS* Constitution *moored in Boston. She is the oldest warship afloat.*

FLASH

• *Merrimack* had a length of 83.8m (275ft), a beam of 11.7m (38ft) and a draught of 6.7m (22ft).

• The conversion of the *Merrimack* into an ironclad cost $172,000 and took almost a year to complete.

• After she had been converted, the ship had an estimated top speed of nine knots, but in reality could manage about six.

• Once a delight to handle, the converted ship was a nightmare to steer, taking around 40 minutes to execute a 180-degree turn.

• A problem with the converted ship was that as she used up her coal and stores she rode higher in the water, until eventually unarmoured sections of her hull were exposed.

• The CSS *Virginia* was the flagship of the James River Squadron.

26. Wood backing to armour
27. 50mm (1.9in) railroad iron laid horizontally
28. 50mm (1.9in) railroad iron laid vertically
29. Gunport and cover
30. Chain to raise cover
31. Shell room
32. Powder store
33. Ship's store
34. Confederate ensign
35. Steering chain
36. Iron cover plate for steering chain
37. Two-bladed 5m (16ft)-diameter Griffiths propeller
38. Rudder

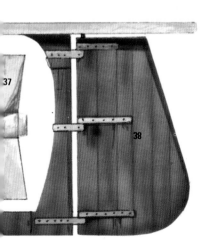

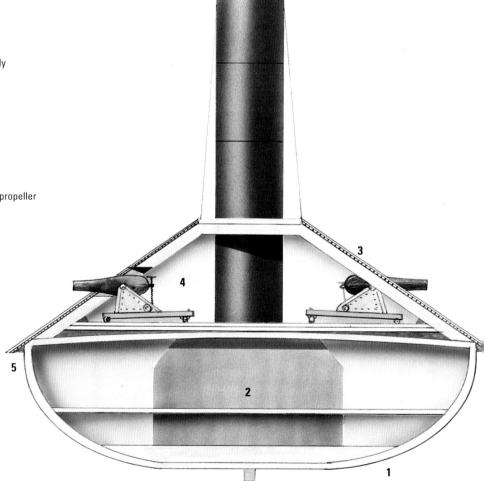

ABOVE: A cross-section of the Merrimack/Virginia after conversion. The original wooden hull (1) was retained, as were the boiler (2) and the engines. The Confederates constructed the armoured superstructure (3) that enclosed the gun deck (4). Note the 'knuckle' (5), an overlap on the superstructure to protect against gunfire and enemy rams.

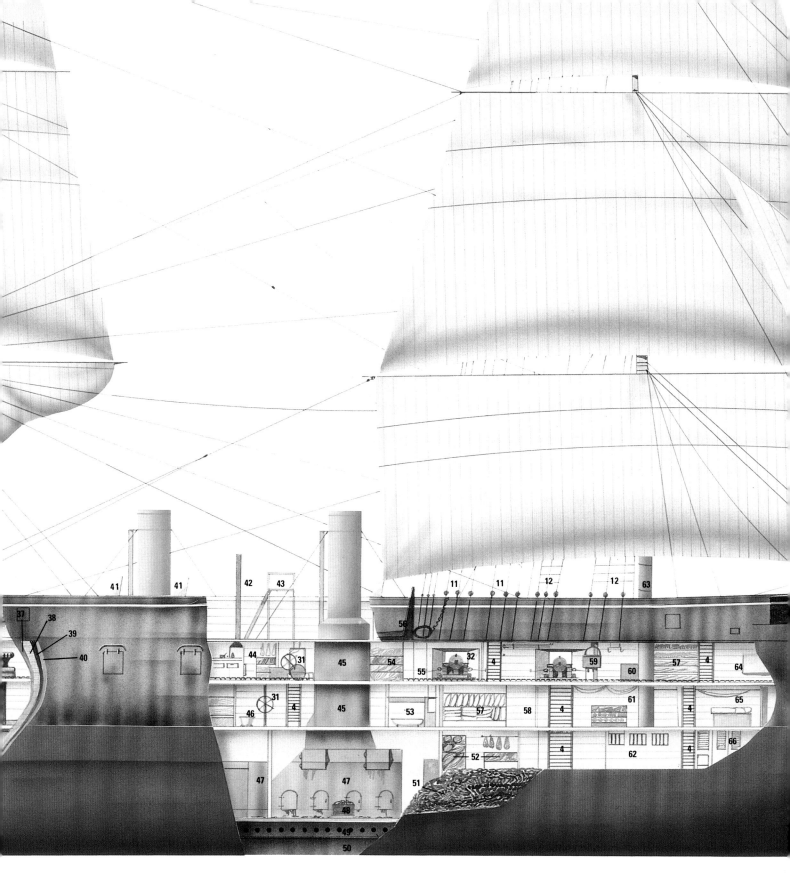

37 38 39 40 41 41 42 43 44 31 45 54 56 11 11 12 12 63 32 4 59 60 57 4 64

31 46 4 45 53 57 58 4 61 4 65

47 47 52 51 4 62 4 66

48 49 50

LEFT: The main steering position. As in earlier ironclads, putting the wheel over was hard work and took a good deal of manpower.

13
12
15
16
11
12
12
34
14
17
19
20
35
18
21
33
3
32
22
4
23
24
30
4
5
4
31
4
4
25
30
26
27
28
29
10

RIGHT: Warrior's gundeck arrangement when she was completed had four 110-pounder BLRs and 13 x 68-pounder muzzle-loaders to each broadside. In 1867 this was changed to ten 178mm (7in) MLRs and two 203mm (8in) MLRs per side.

WARRIOR

During the Crimean War of 1853-56, France constructed, and successfully deployed, armoured floating batteries – iron-plated wooden-hulled craft that were in reality artillery platforms that could pound shorebased targets while remaining proof from Russian onshore shellfire. Britain also built a number of these vessels but these did not take part in any fighting. The next logical step was to armour sea-going warships. Britain was loath to do this as it would make her superior fleet obsolete. France, however, built Gloire. *This forced Britain's hand and she replied with the magnificent* Warrior.

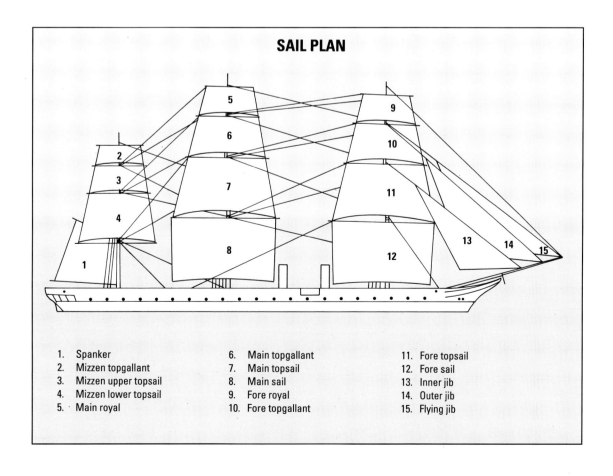

SAIL PLAN

1. Spanker
2. Mizzen topgallant
3. Mizzen upper topsail
4. Mizzen lower topsail
5. Main royal
6. Main topgallant
7. Main topsail
8. Main sail
9. Fore royal
10. Fore topgallant
11. Fore topsail
12. Fore sail
13. Inner jib
14. Outer jib
15. Flying jib

1. Flagstaff holder
2. Stern light
3. Rudder
4. Screw
5. Mizzen mast
6. Conning tower
7. Bridge
8. Officers' quarters
9. Helming position
10. Access to conning tower
11. Ready-to-use ammunition rack
12. Companionway
13. Master-at-arms' quarters
14. Officers' stores
15. Mast foundation
16. Clothing supplies
17. Damage control material
18. Galley stove
19. Engineers' mess
20. Engineers' provisions
21. Ship's stores
22. Dispensary
23. Propeller shaft
24. Shaft alley

25. Engine room
26. Bilge pump
27. Main mast
28. Entry port
29. Ventilator
30. Ventilator to gun deck
31. Steam pipe
32. Funnel casing
33. Armour belt
34. Wooden hull
35. Wooden backing to armour
36. Coal bunker
37. Funnel uptake
38. Steam pipe to engine
39. Boilers
40. Keel
41. Small arms store
42. Capstan
43. Fresh water tanks
44. Bread store
45. Chain locker
46. Lamp room
47. Sail store
48. Petty officers' quarters
49. Fore mast
50. Crew's quarters
51. Sailmakers' workroom

52. Carpenters' workroom
53. Magazine
54. Anchor
55. Anchor rest (cathead)
56. Anchor ports
57. Prow
58. Bowsprit
59. Safety net

FLASH

• Gloire's armour consisted of 110mm (4.3in) plates around the battery on the upper strake, and 120mm (4.7in) plates on and below the waterline. The plates were backed by 660mm (26in) of oak, and fixed to it with screws 560mm (22in) long and 430mm (16in) in diameter. In all, the armour weighed some 830 tons.

• Her two-cylinder, horizontal-return connecting rod (HRCR) engine produced 900 nominal horsepower/2,537 indicated horsepower, and drove a single six-bladed propeller some 5.8m (19ft) in diameter at 51 revolutions per minute for a maximum speed of 13.5 knots. Gloire carried 664 tons of coal.

• Gloire was armed with 34 x Model 1860 160mm (6.2in)/16.7 calibre breech-loading rifled guns, which weighed 3.6 tons each and fired 45kg (99lb) shells; later two more, firing ahead and astern, were added. With a comparatively low muzzle velocity, they were not effective against armour such as Warrior's.

LEFT: Reine Blanche, *one of the Alma class of French second-class battleships of the 1860s. Laid down in 1865, launched in March 1868 and completed in 1869, like* Gloire, *she was a wooden-hulled vessel with iron armour plating. However, she was considerably smaller (and cheaper), at 3,844 tons displacement, and was intended for service on foreign stations.*

RIGHT: Gloire *and her sisters,* Invincible *and* Normandie, *were laid down in 1858, as was the all-iron-hulled frigate* Couronne. *The following year, France started on two two-decker wooden-hulled ironclads, displacing 6,724 tons. These were* Magenta, *which was laid down on 22 June 1859 and launched on 22 June 1861, and* Solférino *(pictured right), which was laid down on 24 June 1859 and launched on 24 June 1861.*

GLOIRE

*S**he never fired her guns in anger, her career was
quite undistinguished, and even her most fervent
admirers never called her beautiful, while her
designer himself admitted from the first that she was a dead-
end, but Gloire will live forever in maritime history, simply
because she was the first true seagoing armoured battleship.
For a brief period she was the most powerful fighting
machine in the world by virtue of her 110-120 millimetres
(4.3-4.7in) of wrought-iron armour plate. She was not a
real novelty, however; there was nothing about her design
that was in any way innovative, and neither was she
entirely suited for operations outside sheltered waters, for
her main battery was only 1.9 metres (6ft 2in) above the
mean waterline. Nonetheless, when the British came to
hear of her existence, Gloire caused a scare which had far-
reaching consequences for an Admiralty which thought itself
invincible. Suddenly, an entirely new race was being run –
and the British did not even have a starter.*

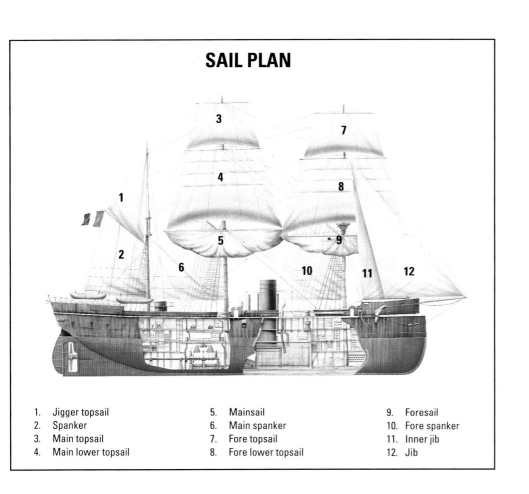

SAIL PLAN

1. Jigger topsail	5. Mainsail	9. Foresail
2. Spanker	6. Main spanker	10. Fore spanker
3. Main topsail	7. Fore topsail	11. Inner jib
4. Main lower topsail	8. Fore lower topsail	12. Jib

FLASH

• *Warrior* displaced 9,210 tons, was 115.8 metres (380ft) long, with a beam of 17.8 metres (58ft), and drew almost eight metres (26ft) of water. Her complement consisted of 707 personnel.

• So that her requirements as a steamer did not interfere with her abilities under sail, *Warrior*'s propeller could be disengaged and lifted out of the water. For the same reason, her funnels were telescopic and could be lowered when she was under sail only.

• *Warrior* cost £377,292 to build. The wooden steam frigate Undaunted, which was launched in the same week as *Warrior*, cost less than a third of this at £105,000.

• *Warrior* was well known for her magnificent figurehead (above right), as was her sister ship *Black Prince*. These were the last ever figureheads to be fitted to British capital ships apart from that mounted on *Rodney* (1884). In 1868 *Warrior* lost her figurehead in a collision with *Royal Oak*, the structure ending up in the latter's gun room.

1. Gig
2. 110-pounder Armstrong breech-loader
3. Captain's quarters
4. Companionway
5. Officers' mess/Sleeping quarters
6. Rudder
7. Frame for lifting screw
8. Screw
9. Waterproof screw boss
10. Shaft
11. Running rigging
12. Shrouds
13. Mizzen mast
14. Main helming position
15. Binnacle
16. Aft bridge
17. Rifle-proof conning tower
18. Upper deck
19. Capstan (auxiliary)
20. Bulwarks
21. Skylight
22. Main deck
23. Emergency steering position

24. Musical instrument room
25. Lower deck
26. Bread room
27. Watertight door
28. Engine room
29. Shot room
30. Sail rack
31. Hand-operated bilge pump
32. 68-pounder smooth bore muzzle-loader
33. Marlin spike rack
34. Main mast
35. Ship's boat
36. Main capstan (to bow anchor)
37. Iron framing to hull
38. Wood backing to hull
39. Iron hull
40. Iron 114mm (4.4in)-thick hull armour
41. Ventilator
42. Pipe from galley
43. Fore bridge
44. Galley
45. Funnel casing
46. Ship's bath (for crew)

47. Boiler
48. Coal truck
49. Double bottom
50. Keel
51. Coal bunker
52. Food store
53. Engineers' bath
54. Bag rack (for crew's possessions)
55. Capstan chain to bow
56. Anchor
57. Stores
58. Engineers' berth area
59. Dining table (partly raised)
60. Water tank
61. Dispenser's stores
62. Prison
63. Fore mast
64. Sailing master's cabin
65. Sick bay
66. Gunners' room
67. Bowsprit
68. Figurehead

LEFT: Even while the last of Italy's diagonal turret ships, Andrea Doria, was being fitted out, the design of large warships was changing: the main armament was now carried on the fore and after decks. The Italian battleship Sardegna (pictured left) was built on this design, entering service a mere four years after Andrea Doria.

23
24
22
25
4
43
26
27
15
20
13
16
21
17
17
6 6 6 6
18 18
6 6
19
12
28
31
30
29
32

RIGHT: The Italian iron-hulled armoured
steam corvette Formidabile. She entered
service in 1862 carrying her sixteen 160mm
(6.2in) guns in batteries down each side, as
in sailing warships. As guns became
bigger less of them were required, and
between 1865 and 1885 navies
experimented with central battery ships in
which the armament was concentrated in
an armoured section towards the centre of
the ship, and diagonal turret ships.

ANDREA DORIA

A ndrea Doria *was the last of the Italian diagonal turret battleships. She belonged to the three-ship* Ruggiero di Lauria *class, which also contained* Francesco Morosini *and* Ruggiero di Lauria *herself. Like the earlier* Duilio *and* Dandolo, *these ships were protected by central-section armour but were steel, rather than iron, hulled and carried breech-loading, rather than muzzle-loading, guns in new style turrets.* Andrea Doria's *complement consisted of 17 officers and 489 men.*

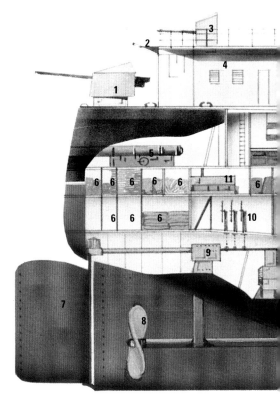

1. 152mm (6in) gun
2. Blast screen
3. 120mm (4.7in) gun
4. Officers' quarters
5. Aft torpedo room
6. Cellular compartments to confine the effects of waterline damage (used for storage)
7. Balanced rudder
8. Screw
9. Steering gear
10. Emergency hand steering gear
11. Air compressor
12. Auxiliary engine for steering gear
13. Wardroom
14. Searchlight platform
15. Captain's cabin
16. Galley
17. Stores
18. Aft magazine for secondary guns
19. Machine room
20. Anti-torpedo net (in stowed position)
21. Boom for anti-torpedo net (in stowed position)
22. Aft bridge
23. Boat-handling derrick
24. Funnel casing
25. Flying bridge
26. Gun hood
27. Glacis plate
28. Aft boiler room
29. Double bottom

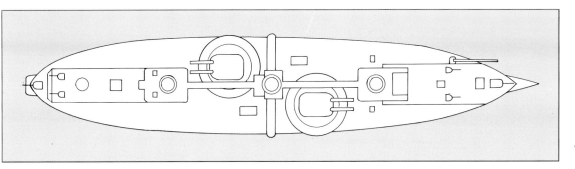

LEFT: A plan view of Andria Do
showing the deck layout. In Ita
diagonal turret ships the starbo
turret was always forward of th
port turret; in Royal Navy ships
reverse was the case.

FLASH

...is engraving of HMS
...tion *clearly shows the 'cul-
...in the after part of the
...ork. This feature was to
...e guns of the after turret to
...essed when firing astern.*
*LEFT: Devastation at speed.
...tion's two direct-acting
...nk engines gave the ship a
...ed of 13.4 knots. She was the
...ish warship to be fitted with
...gines, and these were later
...ged for triple-expansion
...: BELOW: Devastation's
...hip Thunderer photographed
...90s after modernisation.
...e-masted sailing ship in the
...ound is probably HMS*

• *Devastation* was 93.6m (307ft) long overall. She had a beam of 19m (62ft 3in), drew 8.4m (27ft 5in) after her 1891 refit, and was the first iron ship ever built in the Royal Navy's Portsmouth Dockyard. She was laid down on 12 November 1869, launched on 12 July 1871, and completed on 19 April 1873, having been commissioned that January. She was placed in Reserve in 1902 and removed from the Effective List in 1907.

• *Devastation* cost £361,438 to build, and fetched £21,700 when she was sold for breaking up on 12 May 1908. Her sister *Thunderer* (launched 25 March 1872), cost £7,000 more; she was sold on 13 July 1909 for £19,500.

• *Devastation* carried over 1,722 tons of coal, enough to give her a range of 8,700 kilometres (4,578 nautical miles) – an unheard of figure at the time. She was described as 'an impregnable piece of fortification mounted on a floating coal mine'.

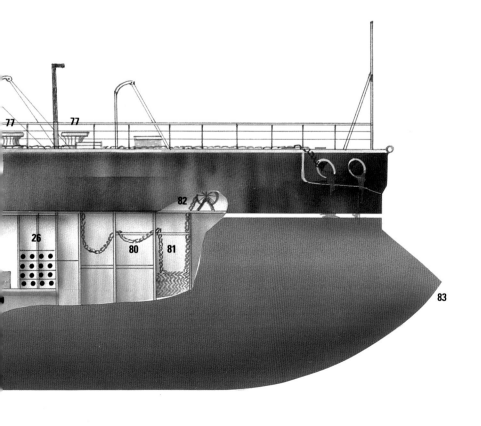

DEVASTATION

*T*he transition from wooden sailing ships with broadside armament to metal steamships with their guns in turrets or barbettes took only a few decades in all, and so innovations in design and technology came thick and fast. Often transitional warships were ridiculed by conservative naval officers and politicians alike, and it is true that some were not up to the task in hand; indeed some, like the ill-fated Captain, which rolled over and sank on 7 September 1870, were disasters. Laid down in the year before the Captain tragedy, and also designed with a very low freeboard, Devastation was generally condemned when she joined the fleet. But, as one noted authority on battleship design has written, 'Certainly, no warship had ever left harbour under such a cloud of pessimism and dismal forebodings as the Devastation; and no warship of such novel design more completely justified all the confidence reposed in her by her constructors.'

1. Rudder
2. Screw
3. Skylights
4. Cordage
5. Vegetable store
6. Officers' store
7. Emergency steering position
8. Galley
9. Lamp room
10. Spirit store
11. Petty officers' store
12. Wing compartments
13. Captain's day cabin
14. Captain's lounge/study
15. Captain's bedroom
16. Wardroom
17. Petty officers' wardroom
18. Passageway
19. Doors to officers' cabins
20. Ship's office
21. Companionway
22. Flour store
23. Chain store
24. Engineers' stores
25. Machine shop
26. Marines' quarters
27. Ship's stores
28. Glacis plate

29. Turret armour
30. Wood backing
31. Frame
32. Sighting hood
33. Recoil exhaust water tank
34. 35-ton 305mm (12in) muzzle-loading rifled gun (in reloading position)
35. Gun carriage
36. Recoil cylinder
37. Elevating beam
38. Reversing gear
39. Elevating ram
40. Roller path
41. Hydraulic loading rams
42. Hydraulic machinery for loading rams
43. Marines' quarters
44. Hammock racks
45. Engine room
46. Lubricating tank
47. Water tank for boilers
48. Fighting top
49. Boat boom
50. Launch
51. Flying bridge
52. Cutter
53. Entry to superstructure
54. Funnel uptake
55. Boiler

56. Double bottom
57. Conning tower
58. Ship's boat
59. Main steering position
60. Fire grate
61. Ashpit
62. Base of side armour (also serves as bilge keel)
63. 305mm (12in)-thick side armour
64. 457mm (17.9in)-thick wood backing
65. Coal bunker
66. Navigation bridge
67. Bridge
68. Entry port to barbette
69. Crew's quarters
70. Carpenter's workroom
71. Steam machinery for turret
72. Repeat panel from bridge
73. Emergency coal bunker
74. Bilge tank
75. Breastwork
76. Anchor
77. Capstan
78. Davit foundation
79. Fresh water tank
80. Anchor cable cleaning tank
81. Anchor cable well
82. Anchor cable engine
83. Ram

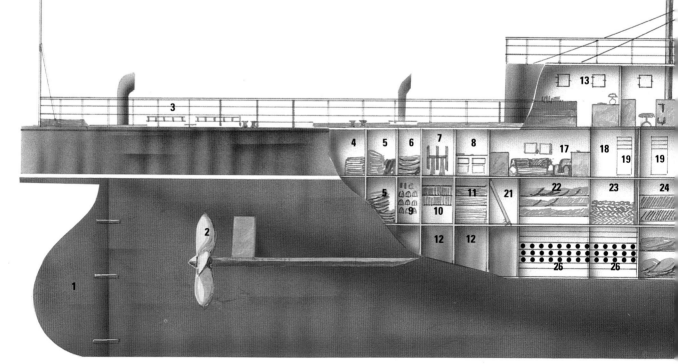

GREAT MEN OF THE SEA

THE FATHER OF THE ITALIAN NAVY

If one man alone can be credited with the construction of the first Italian Navy in the years following unification, then that man must be Benedetto Brin (1833-1898). A naval engineer by trade, Brin was appointed Under-secretary of State by the Minister of Marine, Admiral Saint-Bon, and succeeded to the Ministry on 25 March 1876. From his advantageous position of unprecedented power, working first with Saint-Bon as his naval guide and mentor and, later, on his own, Brin set about constructing an integrated Italian Navy, able to operate as an organic whole.

As well as initiating the Duilio, Italia and Lauria-class diagonal-turret cruisers, he was also responsible for the design studies that led to the introduction of the range of so-called light cruisers which culminated in the Garibaldi class of 8,100-ton displacement ships, as well as the commissioning of a range of smaller destroyers and torpedo boats.

Brin's absorption with the Navy as a whole, and not just with the efficiency of its ships and men, led him to pay close attention, too, to the shipyards, foundries and armouries. When he left the Ministry of Marine in 1887 to take up the post of Minister for Foreign Affairs, he left behind him an Italian Navy that was strong and efficient, and well-supported by shipbuilding and maintenance facilities.

In 1905, seven years after his death at the age of 65, the heavy cruiser *Benedetto Brin* (designed by Brin, but modified after his death by Eng. Admiral Alfredo Micheli) was named after him, as was the Brin-class heavy submarine of 1938-39.

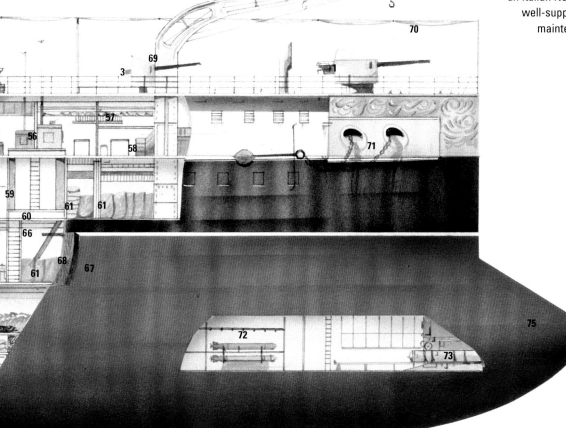

30. Bilge keel	43. Main armament – two 431mm (17in) Armstrong guns	54. Crew area	seawater for use in boilers
31. Engine room		55. Winch	66. Armoured deck
32. Shaft	44. Access tube to flying bridge and fighting top	56. Galley	67. Armour belt
33. Water feed pumps		57. Hammock rack	68. Wood backing to armour
34. Coal bunkers	45. Fighting top	58. Engine for crane	69. Crane for heavy lifting
35. Magazine to main armament	46. Machine guns	59. Access area	70. Awning (folded)
36. Ammunition hoist	47. Ammunition handling room	60. Combing round hatch – to prevent water spilling below	71. Hawsers
37. Steam and hydraulic training gear	48. Fore boiler room		72. Fore torpedo room stowage area
38. Turntable	49. Funnel uptake	61. Food store	73. Fore torpedo tube
39. Elevating mechanism	50. Bridge	62. Lubricating oil store	74. Prow
40. Slide	51. Navigation platform	63. Engine for working winch	75. Ram
41. Rammer	52. Petty officers' quarters	64. Feed water tank for boilers	
42. Ramp to load shell and charges	53. Crew's quarters (stokers)	65. Filter pump – for purifying	

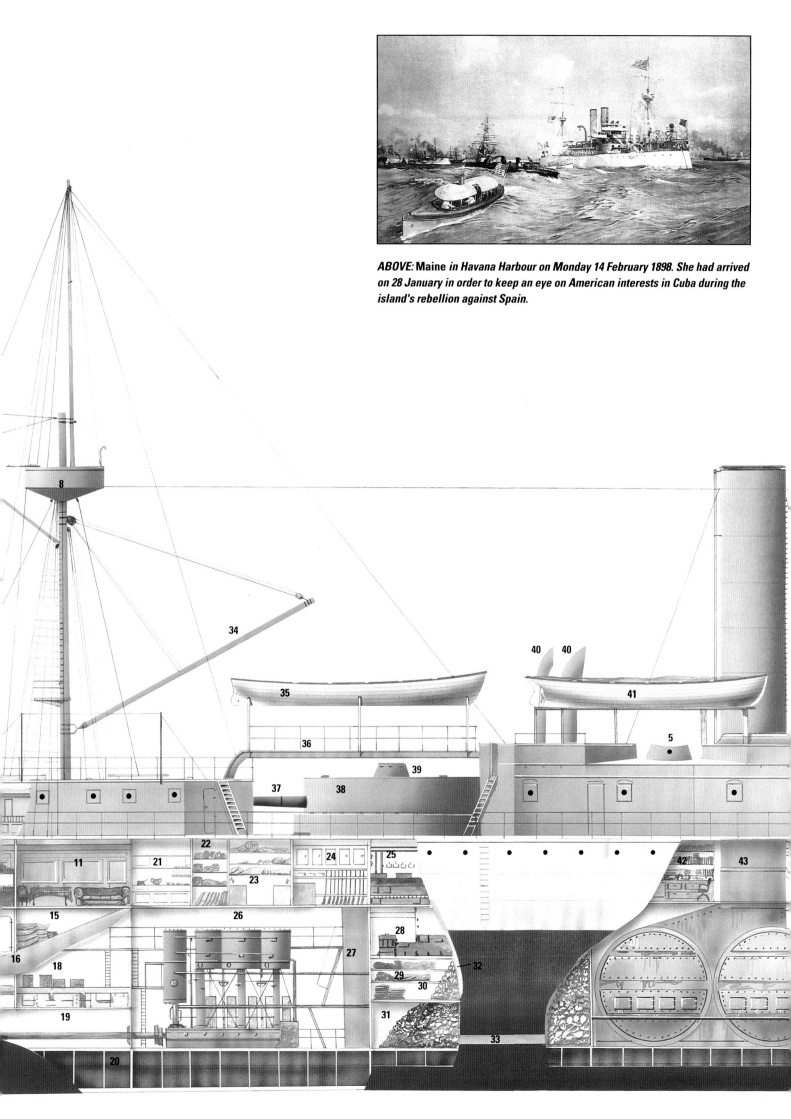

ABOVE: Maine *in Havana Harbour on Monday 14 February 1898. She had arrived on 28 January in order to keep an eye on American interests in Cuba during the island's rebellion against Spain.*

Maine's total complement numbered 354 officers and men, 266 of which (2 officers and 264 men) died when the ship blew up at 21.40 on 15 February 1898. The ship was salvaged in early 1912, then towed out and sunk in the Straits of Florida. On Memorial Day 1915, her main mast became a memorial in Arlington National Cemetery, Virginia, USA.

ABOVE: Members of the class of 1902 at the US Naval Academy, Annapolis, are introduced to Holland (SS 1). The boat stayed at the Academy in a training capacity until July 1905. In November 1910, she was stricken from the list and sold for breaking up in June 1913.

HOLLAND VI

*B*etween the contract being awarded and work beginning on John P. Holland's competition-winning experimental submarine, the US Navy changed its mind about the powerplant to be fitted for running on the surface. Holland had specified an Otto gasoline engine; the Navy decided it wanted a pair of small triple-expansion reciprocating steam engines. The inventor warned that the steam engines would make the craft unbearably hot, and that each time the vessel needed to submerge, steam pressure in the boiler would have to be blown off first, an operation of at least ten minutes' duration. He considered that these problems could be the finish of the project, so he abandoned USS Plunger, as the steam boat was to be called, and set about building another craft, which he called Holland VI.

LEFT: One of Simon Lake's submarines, Argonaut, *seen here under construction. His early craft had wheels, but the irregular landscape beneath the sea meant they were of dubious value. Lake eventually succeeded in having some of his later craft accepted by the US Navy. RIGHT: J. P. Holland in the conning tower of* SS 1.

1.	Rudder	
2.	Hydroplane	
3.	Screw guard	
4.	Screw	
5.	Bilge	
6.	Dynamo	
7.	Shaft	
8.	Steering motor	
9.	Exhaust pipe	
10.	Diving engine	
11.	Reduction gear	
12.	Petrol engine	
13.	Ballast tanks	
14.	Flywheel	
15.	Electric motor	
16.	Bilge pump	
17.	Bilge outlet	
18.	Keel plate	
19.	Main ballast tanks	
20.	Electric batteries	
21.	Space for spare torpedo	
22.	Air compressor	
23.	Depth gauge	
24.	Emergency valves	
25.	Diving wheel	
26.	Conning tower	
27.	Sight holes	
28.	Hatch	
29.	Hatch control	
30.	Compensating tank	
31.	Dynamite gun	
32.	Breech	
33.	Fin (stabiliser) to dynamite shell	
34.	Dynamite shell	
35.	Control rod to gun muzzle cap	
36.	Muzzle cap	
37.	Compressed air tank to gun	
38.	Compressed air tank to torpedo tube	
39.	Torpedo tube	
40.	Torpedo	
41.	Control rod to torpedo tube cap	
42.	Torpedo tube cap	
43.	Float to fuel tank	
44.	Fuel tank	
45.	Folding mast	
46.	Mooring cleats	

FLASH

• *Maine* was to have carried a pair of 15-ton second-class torpedo boats. Indeed, one was built but failed to make its design speed of 18 knots by a very considerable margin, and the project was shelved.

• *Maine* was 98.9-metres (324ft 4in) long, had a beam of 17.4 metres (57ft), and drew 6.9 metres (22ft 6in) of water at her standard displacement of 6,682 tons. Her dimensions were limited by the capacity of American harbours and drydocks at that time.

• The ship's fuel capacity was very low for a ship which was originally designed as a cruiser – just 885 tons. It was planned to equip her with a full sailing rig on three masts, but that idea was dropped before she was launched.

• *Maine*'s two engines were the US Navy's first vertically mounted three-cylinder triple-expansion engines. Her design speed was 17 knots.

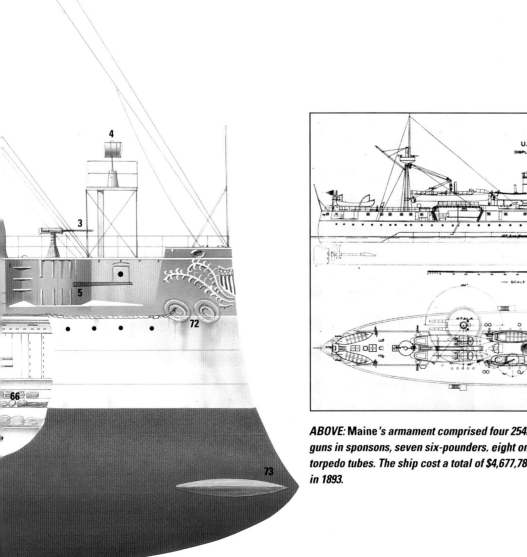

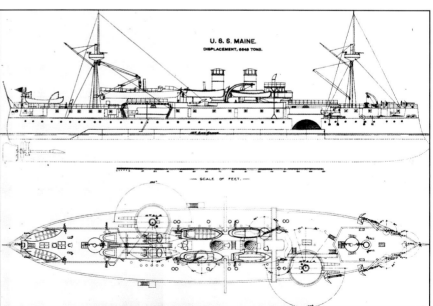

ABOVE: **Maine** *'s armament comprised four 254mm (10in) guns in turrets, six 152mm (6in) guns in sponsons, seven six-pounders, eight one-pounders, four Gatling guns, and four torpedo tubes. The ship cost a total of $4,677,789. The picture is an unofficial plan published in 1893.*

MAINE

The diagonal turret layout of Maine – and Texas – followed a plan developed by the great Italian naval architect Benedetto Brin. After the battle of Lissa in 1866 had reintroduced the ram as an offensive weapon, it became necessary for battleships to be able to lay down heavy fire ahead, and so Brin designed a number of ships (including Duilio/Dandolo and Italia/Lepanto) whose entire main armament could be trained fore or aft, as well as to either broadside. To achieve this, he sited the guns well outside the centreline – diagonally, one forward and one aft – so that each could be fired past the central superstructure. By the time Maine and Texas were completed, the style was outmoded. Nevertheless, the ships made the US Navy a respectable force in the Western Hemisphere.

1. Rudder
2. Screw
3. One-pounder gun
4. Searchlight
5. 152mm (6in) gun
6. Machine gun
7. Steering position
8. Fighting top
9. Captain's cabin
10. Officer's cabin
11. Wardroom
12. Torpedo room
13. Food store
14. Cold store
15. Ship's store
16. Armoured deck
17. Tiller room
18. Steering engine
19. Shaft tunnel
20. Double bottom
21. Galley
22. Pantry
23. Laundry
24. Armoury
25. Turret engine
26. Engine room
27. Lubricating tank
28. Generator
29. Engineers' stores
30. Reserve coal bunker
31. Coal bunker
32. Armour belt
33. Bilge keel
34. Boat boom
35. Cutter
36. Flying bridge
37. 254mm (10in) gun

38. Turret
39. Sighting hood
40. Ventilator
41. Steam cutter
42. Ship's office
43. Funnel uptake
44. Sick bay
45. Boiler room
46. Boat crane
47. Sailing launch
48. Chart house
49. Conning tower
50. Rammer
51. Cradle
52. Turret roller path
53. Ammunition rails
54. Pump room
55. Wing passages
56. Handling room
57. Magazine
58. Machine room
59. Electricians' stores
60. Purser's store
61. Fresh water tank
62. Crew
63. Chain locker
64. Purser's office
65. Bread store
66. Carpenters' store
67. Sail locker
68. General store/Lamp room
69. Capstan
70. Anchor crane
71. Anchor
72. Anchor ports
73. Ram

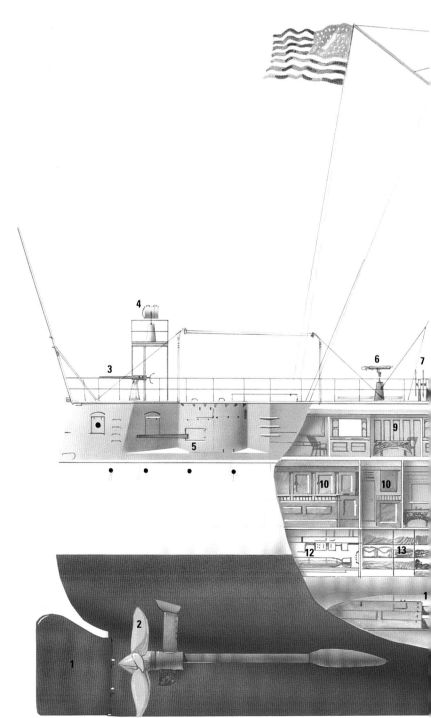

FLASH

- *Holland VI* was 16.3 metres (53ft 4in) long, 3.5 metres (11ft) deep from the bottom of her hull to the top of her conning tower and had a largest diameter of 3.1 metres (10ft). She displaced 64 tons on the surface and 76 tons submerged. Her petrol engine gave her a theoretical range of 2,400 kilometres (1,263 nautical miles) at ten knots on 4,500 litres (17,032 US gallons) of fuel. Using her dynamotor she could manage six knots for 55 kilometres (28 nautical miles). She had a crew of six and a maximum diving depth of 22.8 metres (74ft 8in). Her armament consisted of three Whitehead self-propelled torpedoes, one in the tube and two reloads, as well as six 100-kilogram (220lb) charges for the two Pneumatic Dynamite Guns (one was later removed). The charges were launched by compressed air with the craft just submerged.

- The steam-driven submarine USS *Plunger* – the US Navy prototype for which Holland was awarded the contract – was started at the Columbian Iron Works, Baltimore, USA, and completed at Triggs Iron Works, Richmond, Virginia. This vessel should not be confused with the A class submarine USS *Plunger* (*SS 2*, launched 1902), which was built in Elizabethport, New Jersey.

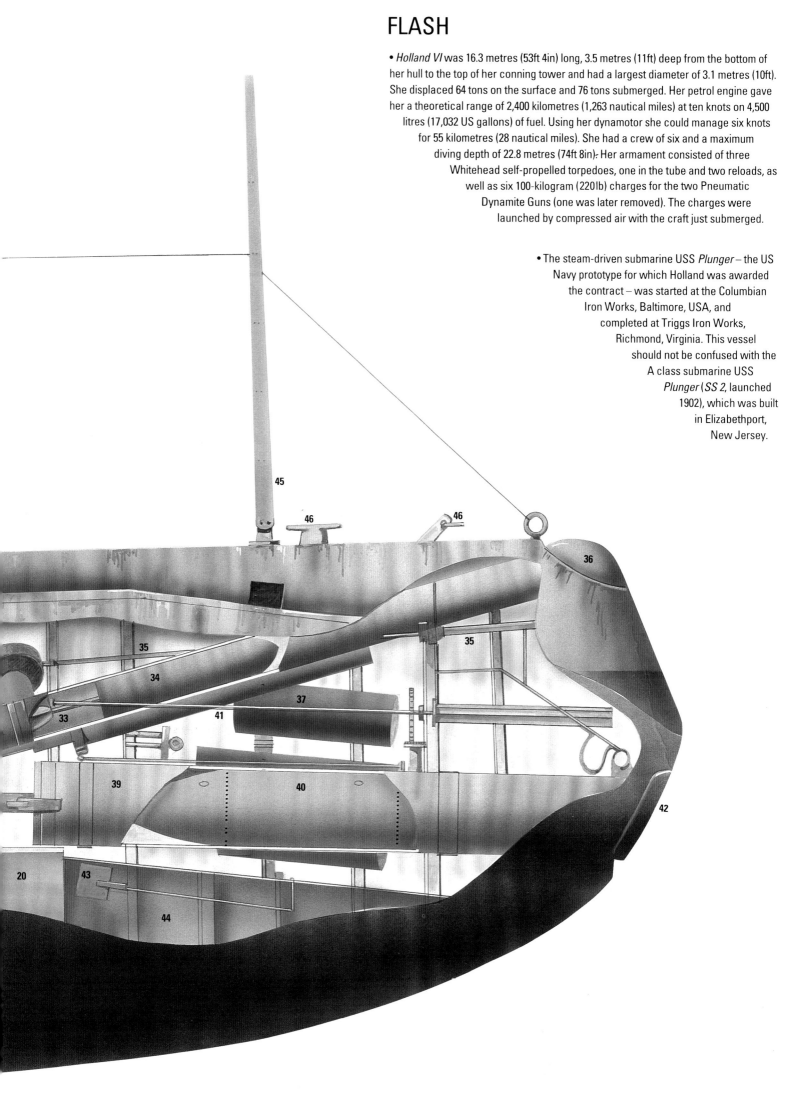

GIUSEPPE
GARIBALDI

G iuseppe Garibaldi *was the eighth ship to be built in the successful Garibaldi class. According to a decree issued by the Italian Ministry of Marine in August 1893, she was to have been the first such vessel, but each of the preceding seven ships were sold to foreign powers before they were off the stocks. Up until that time Italy had relied on foreign production for the supply of all her capital ships. However, the design of the Garibaldi-class vessels was ideally suited to countries with strategic geography akin to that of Italy – a long coastline and little in the way of far-flung overseas possessions – and so the ships were much in demand. It wasn't until April 1901 that the* Giuseppe Garibaldi *was finally commissioned into the Italian Navy.*

LEFT: Giuseppe Garibaldi *making her way under full steam.*

FLASH

• *Dreadnought* measured 160 metres (525ft) overall, with a maximum beam of 25 metres (82ft); she drew 9.4 metres (30ft 8in) of water when fully loaded. The ship's design displacement was 18,110 tons (18,400 tonnes), and her actual displacement, in battle-going order with full crew, stores and fuel was 21,845 tons (22,194 tonnes). HMS *Dreadnought* cost £1,785,683 to build; her sale for scrap in 1921 recouped just £44,750 of that.

• *Dreadnought's* machinery was as revolutionary as her armament, as instead of reciprocating engines she had a four-shaft Parsons geared turbine powerplant – two units in each of the two engine rooms – capable of generating 23,000 shaft horsepower at 320rpm. Fed by 18 Babcock and Wilcox boilers, the engines pushed the ship along at a maximum speed of 21 knots, giving *Dreadnought* a three-knot advantage on the old British battle fleet; indeed they made her the fastest battleship in the world.

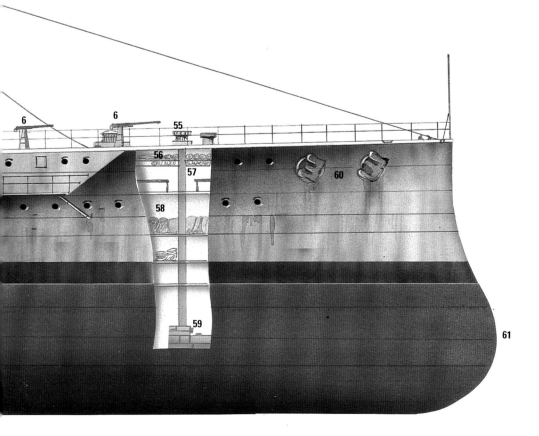

32. Armoured access tube to conning tower
33. Engineers' stores
34. Forward boiler rooms
35. Fuel tanks (oil)
36. Double bottom
37. Manual shell loading control
38. Shell crane
39. Breech
40. Collar support
41. Shell cradle
42. Roller path
43. Shell handling room
44. Barbette wall
45. Ammunition hoist
46. Access to magazines
47. Magazine
48. Shell room
49. Food store
50. Crew's galley
51. Electricians' workshop
52. Dynamo
53. Bilge pump
54. Fresh water tank
55. Capstan
56. Hammock stowage
57. Crew's quarters
58. Vegetable store
59. Capstan engine
60. Anchors
61. Ram

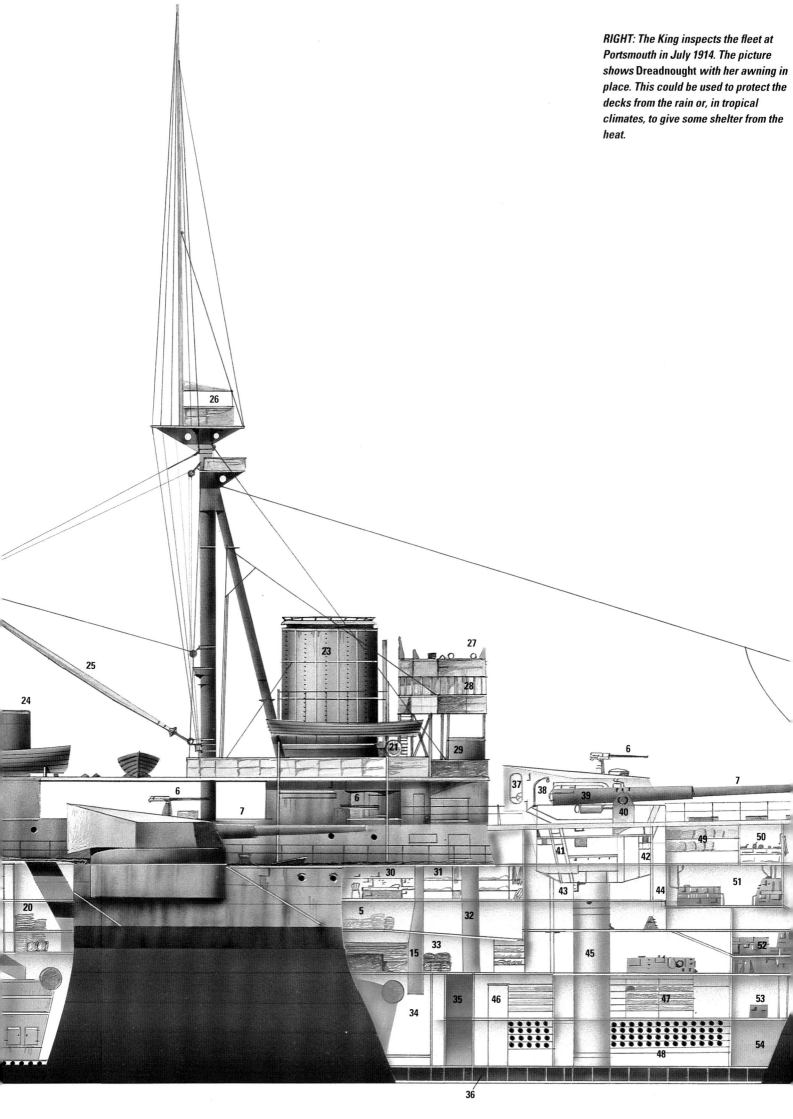

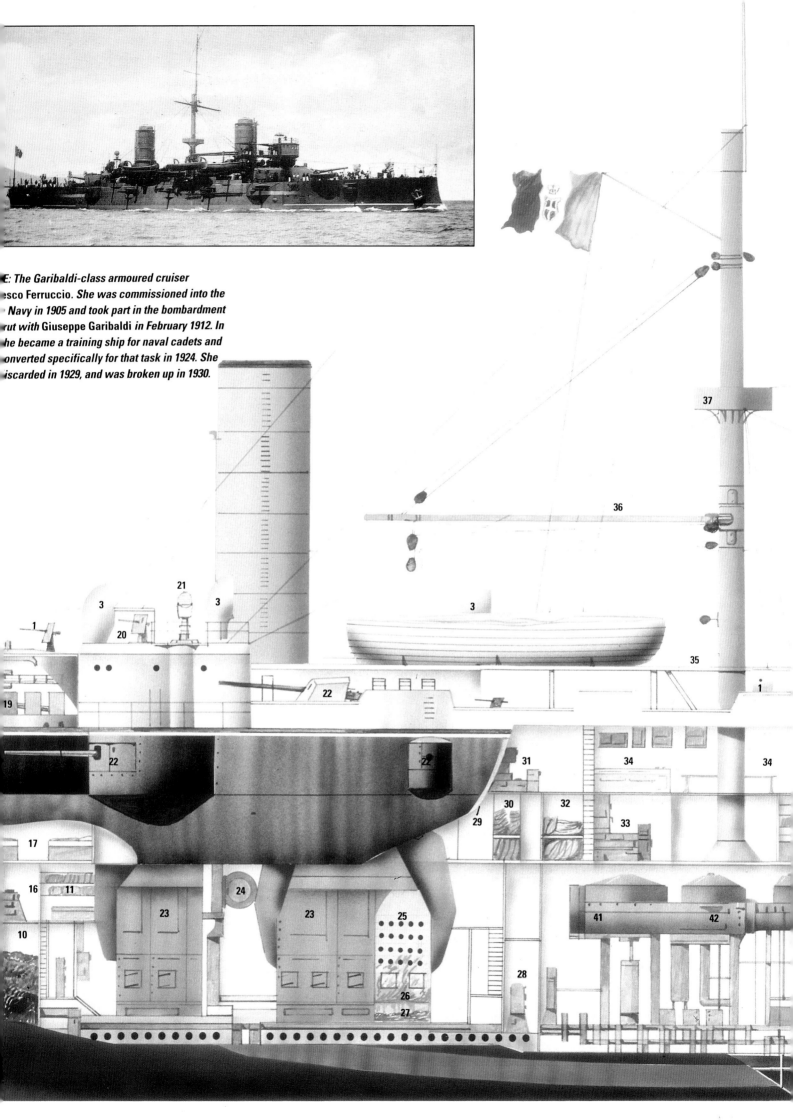

E: The Garibaldi-class armoured cruiser
sco Ferruccio. She was commissioned into the
Navy in 1905 and took part in the bombardment
rut with Giuseppe Garibaldi in February 1912. In
he became a training ship for naval cadets and
onverted specifically for that task in 1924. She
iscarded in 1929, and was broken up in 1930.

ABOVE: The Austrian submarine U4, which sank Giuseppe Garibaldi on 18 July 1915. U4 was built for the Austrian Navy in Germany by Germaniawerft at Kiel, and was launched in November 1908. She was then towed to Pola via Gibraltar for service in the Mediterranean. U4 was the longest serving Austrian submarine. She was scrapped in 1920.

LEFT: Dreadnought *tied up alongside at Portsmouth, with HMS* Victory *and* Gosport *beyond. The diagonal bars fixed at intervals along the hull were used to deploy the anti-torpedo nets. The bars were hinged at their lower ends, while their upper ends were attached to nets stored at deck level. In order to bring the nets into operation the bars were swung out from the side of the vessel. The ship could travel slowly with nets deployed, but if she went too fast they would gather at the stern of the ship and become tangled in the propellers.

DREADNOUGHT

*I*n 1903, in an article in Jane's Fighting Ships *of that year, the Torinese General di Genio Navale Vittorio Cuniberti put forward the idea of battleships giving up their medium-calibre secondary armament in favour of increased main armament. Such 'all-big-gun', or monocalibre, battleships would render existing capital ships obsolete, and were what the Americans, Russians, and Japanese had in mind to build. The Royal Navy had studied the idea, but now they had to act. They needed to beat the other nations to the punch if they were to retain their naval superiority – and they did, with* Dreadnought. *The illustration shows* Dreadnought *as she would have looked around the time of her completion in 1906.*

ABOVE: Dreadnought *after her launch at Portsmouth on 10 February 1906. Less than ten months later she was complete and undergoing acceptance trials. In addition to her ma armament and anti-torpedo guns, she had five submerged 457mm (17.9in) torpedo tubes. Her main armour consisted of a 280mm (11in) main belt, a 203mm (8in) upper main belt and forward and after strakes of 152mm (6in) and 102mm (4in) respectively. There was also 280mm (11in) on the barbettes, turret faces and conning tower, and the decks were also armoured.*

1. Torpedo room
2. Balanced rudder
3. Screw
4. Steering engine
5. Ship's stores
6. 12-pounder gun, 18cwt quick-firing
7. 304mm (11.9in) gun, 45-calibre Mk 10
8. Ventilators to engine room
9. Parsons steam turbine engine
10. Lubricating oil tank
11. Aft lookout station
12. Anti-torpedo net boom
13. Anti-torpedo net
14. Coal bunker
15. Boiler room ventilators
16. Oil tank (oil was sprayed onto the burning coal to increase performance)
17. Boiler
18. Furnace
19. Ash pit
20. Cordage store
21. Searchlight
22. Steam pipe
23. Funnel casing
24. Aft conning station
25. Boom
26. Main lookout station/Spotting top
27. Upper bridge
28. Bridge and navigation plotting room
29. Conning tower
30. Sick bay
31. Engineers' quarters

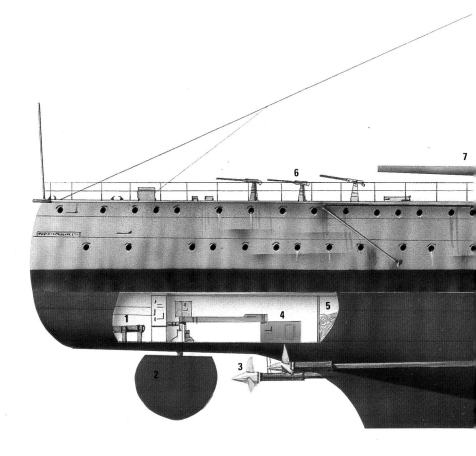

12-pounder gun
Auxiliary ventilator
Main ventilator
Wardroom
Officers' pantry
Officers' quarters
Rudder
Screw
Main steering engine
Coal store
Ship's stores
Emergency hand steering
Dynamo
203mm (8in) ammunition room
Engine for aft turret
Electricians' room
Sick bay
203mm (8in) gun
Ready ammunition holders
Aft conning position
Searchlight
152mm (6in) gun
Niclausse boilers
Forced draught
Boiler tubes
Furnace
Ashpit
Bilge pump
152mm (6in)-thick central armour belt
Boatswain's stores
Machine shop
Vegetable store
Boom engine
Crew
Boat deck
Boom
Fighting top
Compass platform
Galley
Issuing room

41. High-pressure cylinder
42. Medium-pressure cylinder
43. Low-pressure cylinder
44. Oil filter
45. Clothes store
46. Flour store
47. Funnel uptake
48. Feed water tanks
49. Triple bottom
50. Upper bridge
51. Navigation bridge
52. Conning tower
53. Chart room
54. Access tube to conning tower
55. Carpenters' stores
56. Oil tank
57. Fresh water
58. 254mm (10in) 45-calibre gun
59. Recoil cylinder
60. Shell tray
61. Turntable
62. Shell hoist
63. Shell handling room
64. Main hoist
65. Access doors
66. 254mm (10in) ammunition magazine
67. Cordite room
68. Armourers' stores/Work space
69. Capstan

70. Crew sleeping area
71. Awning store
72. Capstan engine
73. Armoured deck (sloping at sides and to bow and stern; meets bottom of armoured belt)
74. 76mm (3in)-thick armour belt at bow and stern
75. Lamp room
76. Paint store
77. Cordage
78. Chain store
79. Anchor port
80. Ram

FLASH

• In all, ten Garibaldi-class armoured cruisers were built in Italy between 1893 and 1905. From *Cristóbal Colon* onwards, all ships in the class carried the same secondary armament, which consisted of fourteen 152mm (6in) quick-firing guns, ten 76mm (3in) guns, six 74mm (2.9in) cannon, two machine guns and four 450mm (17.7in) torpedo tubes. As for their main armament, *Giuseppe Garibaldi*, *Varese* and *Francesco Ferruccio* all carried a single 254mm (10in) gun in the fore turret and two 203mm (8in) guns in the aft turret, but the ships sold for export had variations on this theme.

• The Garibaldi-class ships were 111 metres (364ft) long overall, with a beam of 18.2 metres (60ft), and a full load displacement of 8,100 tons. With coal reserves of 1,180 tons, the Garibaldi class had a range of 17,250km (9,079 nm) at 10 knots, and 10,200 km (5,368 nm) at 16 knots.

• At the time, the general fleet required a top speed of around 20 knots, and all the Garibaldi-class ships comfortably exceeded 19 knots, with *Varese* actually reaching 20 knots.

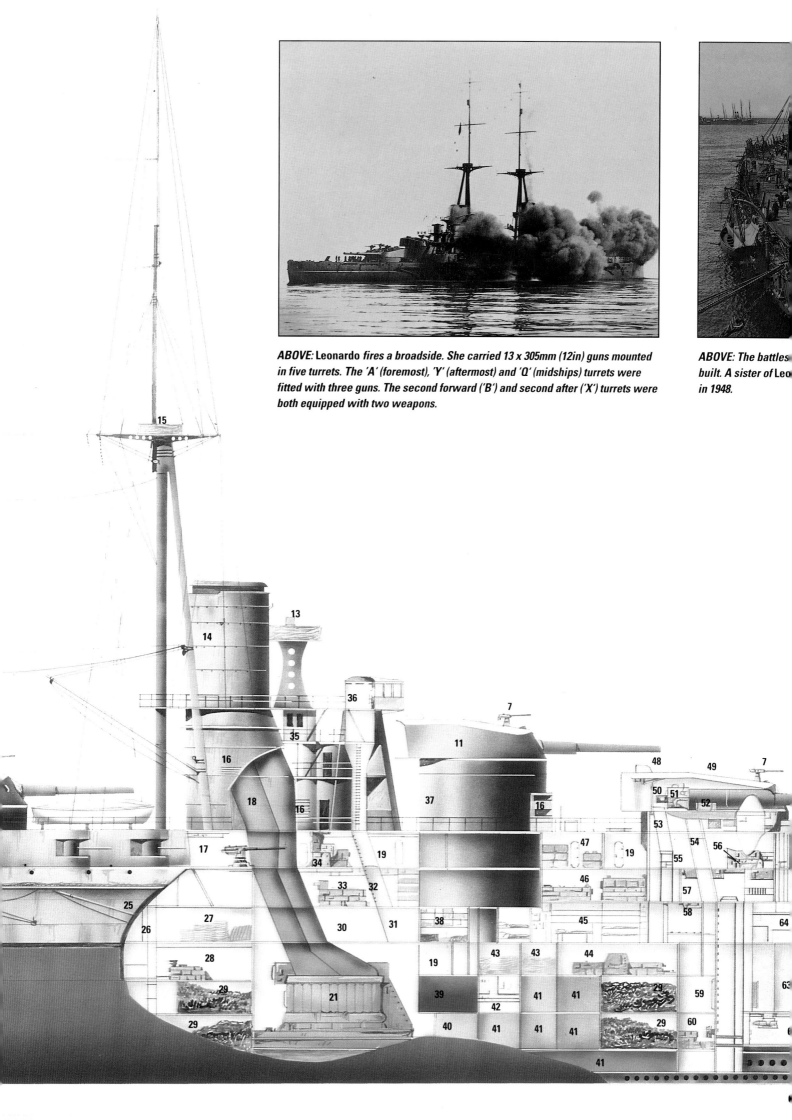

ABOVE: Leonardo fires a broadside. She carried 13 x 305mm (12in) guns mounted in five turrets. The 'A' (foremost), 'Y' (aftermost) and 'Q' (midships) turrets were fitted with three guns. The second forward ('B') and second after ('X') turrets were both equipped with two weapons.

ABOVE: The battles
built. A sister of Leo
in 1948.

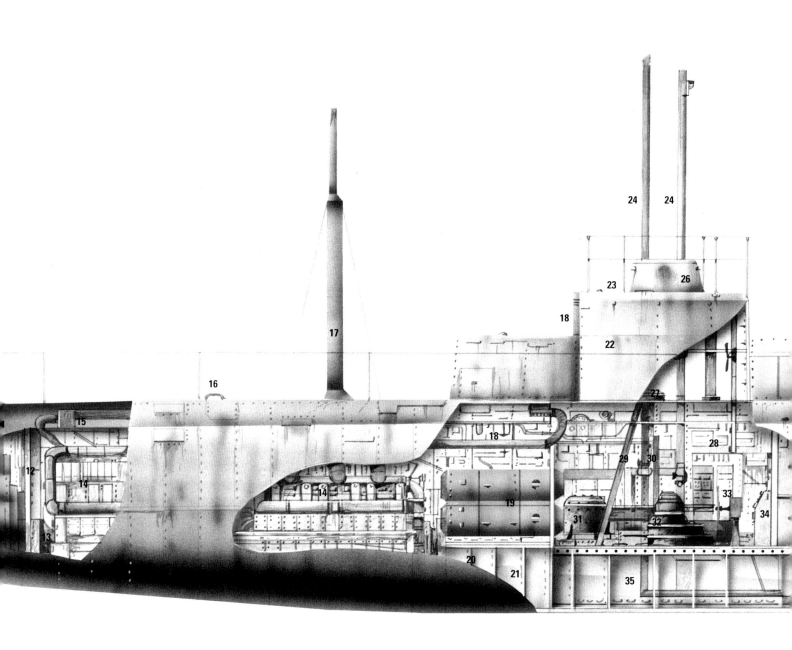

ABOVE: The German U-boat base at Wilhelmshaven, pictured in 1915. Early successes by German submarines against British warships led to deep anxiety in the Royal Navy about the Grand Fleet's vulnerability to U-boat attack.

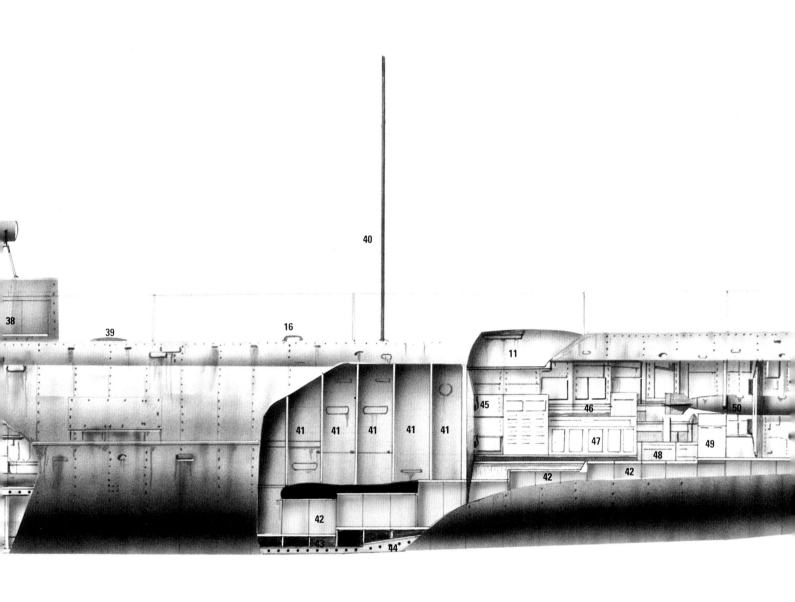

38

39

16

40

11

45

46

50

41 41 41 41 41

47

49

48

42 42

42

43 44

LEFT: Kapitän-Leutnant Otto Weddigen (1882-1915), commander of U9 when she sank Aboukir and her sisters, and HMS Hawke. On the day U9 sank the three British cruisers, the swell prevented lookouts from seeing the submarine's periscope. On 18 March 1915, when commanding U29, Weddigen was not so lucky. His periscope was spotted aboard the battleship HMS Dreadnought, which then ran his boat down.

ABOVE: The crew of U9. Weddigen – nicknamed the 'Polite Pirate' by the British – is in the centre of the picture.

ABOVE: A stern view of the Cavour-class single-calibre battleship Leonardo da Vinci. Her armour weighed over 4,900 tonnes in total and included a 254mm (10in)-thick belt and 111mm (4.3in) of protection on the battery deck. The ship carried a complement of 35 officers and around 1,200 men.

LEONARDO DA VINCI

*T*he battleship Leonardo da Vinci *and her sisters in the Cavour class,* Giulio Cesare *and* Conte di Cavour *herself, formed the first full group of Italian dreadnoughts – or single-calibre battleships. Such 'all-big-gun' battleships, in which medium-calibre secondary armament was sacrificed to accommodate more heavy guns, had first been suggested by the Italian General Vittorio Cuniberti in an article published in the 1903 edition of* Jane's Fighting Ships. *The idea was first given substance in the form of HMS* Dreadnought *(1906). Italy had to wait until 1913 for her first dreadnought type, the 21,600-ton* Dante Alighieri, *to be completed. She was the first ship in the world to carry her large-calibre guns in triple turrets, starting a trend which was continued in the Cavour class, and later in the Doria class.*

1. Stern anchor port
2. Rudder
3. Screw
4. Steering engine
5. Internal armoured deck (sloping at stern and sides)
6. Turret with three 305mm (12in), 46-calibre guns
7. 14-pounder, 50-calibre gun
8. Shelf for anti-torpedo nets
9. Anti-torpedo net
10. Boom for anti-torpedo net
11. Turret with two 305mm (12in), 46-calibre guns
12. Aft conning position
13. Searchlight
14. Funnel casing
15. Lookout station
16. Ventilators
17. Secondary battery deck
18. Funnel uptakes
19. Access corridor
20. Engineers' stores
21. Boilers
22. Engines
23. Boat deck
24. Boat boom

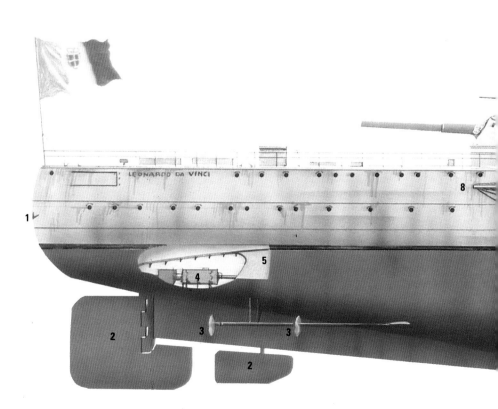

FLASH

• In the action against *Aboukir*, *Hogue* and *Cressy*, it took exactly one hour for one primitive 500-ton submarine to inflict more casualties than Nelson's fleet had suffered at the Battle of Trafalgar.

• Otto Weddigen did not outlast his victims for long. He was given command of *U29*, and rashly tried to attack a formation of battleships of the Grand Fleet on patrol in the North Sea. His periscope was sighted aboard HMS *Dreadnought*, and the 21,844-ton ship swung out of line to ram her tiny opponent. *U29* was sliced open by the *Dreadnought*'s bow and went down with all hands.

• After her surrender, *U9* was being towed from Harwich on the east coast of England to Morecambe on the west in March 1919 when she broke adrift from her tugs and drifted onto the beach near Dover. She was refloated the following month and finished her voyage to Morecambe to be scrapped.

1. Screw (twin, one each side of rudder)	19. Air compressors	39. Escape hatch
2. Rudder	20. Fuel	40. Light mast for signalling
3. Prop shaft	21. Lubricating oil	41. Buoyancy tanks (main)
4. Prop shaft support	22. Conning tower	42. Batteries
5. Aft torpedo tube	23. Platform	43. Double bottom
6. Rudder motor	24. Periscope	44. Keel plate
7. Aft hydroplane	25. Navigation light	45. Watertight door
8. Aft crew quarters	26. Upper hatch	46. Forward crew space
9. Stores	27. Connecting hatch	47. Food stores/Clothing
10. Electric motors	28. Control room	48. Torpedo cartridge stores
11. Torpedo-loading hatch/Escape hatch	29. Ladder to conning tower	49. Galley
12. Bulkhead	30. Periscope controls	50. Spare torpedo
13. Coupling between diesel and electric motors	31. Main bilge pump	51. Forward torpedo tube
14. Diesel engine (pair, back to back)	32. Auxiliary bilge pump	52. Anchor-raising engine
15. Exhaust for surface running	33. Vertical control	53. Forward hydroplane
16. Lifting hook	34. Wireless	54. Forward trim tank
17. Exhaust outlet	35. Regulating tank	55. Capstan
18. Air intake	36. Officers' quarters	56. Torpedo door
	37. Searchlight	57. Anchor
	38. Deck spares (ropes, handrail, etc)	

U9

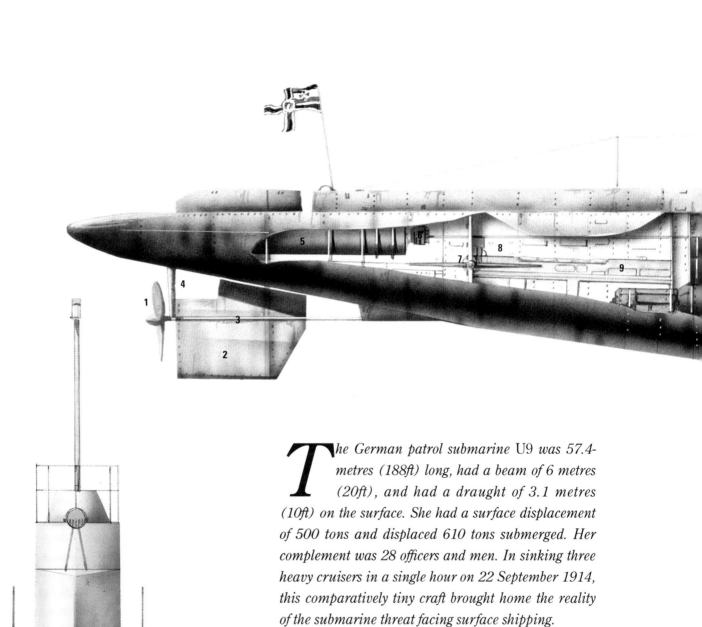

*T*he German patrol submarine U9 was 57.4-metres (188ft) long, had a beam of 6 metres (20ft), and had a draught of 3.1 metres (10ft) on the surface. She had a surface displacement of 500 tons and displaced 610 tons submerged. Her complement was 28 officers and men. In sinking three heavy cruisers in a single hour on 22 September 1914, this comparatively tiny craft brought home the reality of the submarine threat facing surface shipping.

LEFT: A cross-section of U9, taken amidships. Shown are the batteries (1) for the electric motors, the water pumps (2) for filling and emptying the submarine's ballast tanks, the wheel (3) for controlling the submarine's depth, and the diesel engines (4).

FLASH

Cesare *in the Ansaldo yard, Genoa, where she was* *survived both world wars and passed to the USSR*

• *Leonardo da Vinci* and her sisters *Conte di Cavour* and *Giulio Cesare* were designed to displace 24,500 tons at full load. In fact there was a slight variation between the three ships, and their actual displacements were 23,868, 24,410 and 24,287 tons respectively.

• *Leonardo da Vinci*'s bow included the obligatory ram, and her overall length and waterline length were therefore almost identical at 176 metres (577ft). She had a beam of 28 metres (92ft), and drew 9.3 metres (30ft 5in) when fully loaded. Despite producing 1,300 shaft horsepower, she was actually slightly slower than her designed speed of 22 knots, recording a top speed of 21.6 knots.

• The Cavour-class ships could sustain a rate of fire of one round per gun per minute and, since each armour-piercing shell weighed 453kg, could deliver a total of five and a half tons of ordnance in that time.

• All three ships carried 1,450 tons of coal and 850 tons of oil, giving them a range of 1,900km (1,000 nm) at top speed.

25. Armour belt
26. Secondary ammunition hoist
27. Flour store
28. Machine room for secondary battery
29. Coal bunker
30. Wing passage
31. Entry to armoured tube to bridge
32. Armoured access tube to bridge
33. Auxiliary dynamo room
34. Engine room for forward boat boom
35. Navigation platform
36. Conning tower/Day bridge
37. Barbette
38. Boatswain's stores
39. Lubricating oil
40. Fresh water
41. Fuel oil
42. Fuel monitoring point
43. Ship's stores
44. Main dynamo room
45. Dispensary/Sick bay
46. Machine shop
47. Carpenters' store
48. Gun sighting hood
49. Gun hood
50. Gun loading cage
51. Breech power opening cylinder
52. Compressor
53. Secondary hoist
54. Primary hoist
55. Upper shell handling room
56. Turret turning mechanism
57. Ammunition transfer room
58. Turret training limit buffer
59. Cordite cage opening
60. Engine for turret machinery
61. Triple bottom
62. Shell room
63. Cordite room
64. Cold storage for provisions
65. Canvas store
66. Lading tube to shell room
67. Lamp room
68. Cordage
69. Paint and caulking store
70. Crew's quarters
71. Pump room
72. Cellular compartments
73. Capstan winch
74. Capstan
75. Anchor
76. Strengthened ram

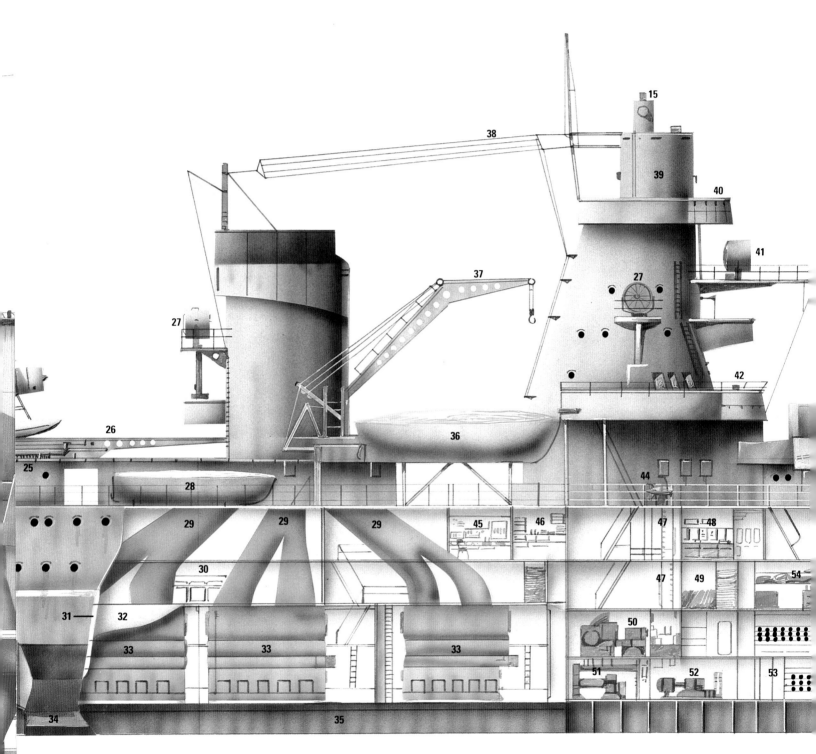

34. Bilge keel	45. Ship's office	56. Radio room
35. Double bottom	46. Dispensary	57. Ammunition-handling room
36. Motor boat	47. Access tunnel to control station	58. Ammunition hoist
37. Boat crane	48. Plotting room	59. Crew's quarters
38. Wireless aerial	49. Flour store	60. Ship's stores
39. Main control station	50. Air-conditioning plant	61. Turret turning engine
40. Observation bridge	51. Pump room	62. Fresh water tanks
41. Remote-controlled searchlight	52. Dynamo	63. Fuel tank
42. Navigation bridge	53. Trim tanks	64. Capstan
43. 150mm (5.9in) 50 calibre gun Mk 10 in single turret	54. Electrical stores	65. Anchor
44. Paravane	55. Chief petty officer's stores	

FLASH

• On completion, *Queen Elizabeth*'s light-load displacement was nearly 30,511 tons. After modifications she had, by 1944, a light-load displacement of 33,956 tons and a deep-load displacement of more than 38,385 tons.

• *Queen Elizabeth*'s engines were four-shaft Parsons turbines, her design speed was 23 knots and she had a range at 10 knots of 7,750 kilometres (4,079 nautical miles).

• In addition to her eight 380mm (15in) guns, the ship originally had 16 x 152mm (152mm) guns. The latter were all later removed and replaced with 20 dual-purpose 114mm (4.4in) quick-firing guns.

• *Queen Elizabeth* was 196.8 metres (645ft 6in) long overall, had a beam of 27.6 metres (90ft 5in) – later increased to 31.7 metres (104ft) with the addition of anti-torpedo bulges – and drew 10 metres (32ft) at full load. Her complement numbered around 950.

ABOVE: An aerial shot of Queen Elizabeth *gives an idea of the great size and power of a superdreadnought battleship. Note she still has her original two funnels. RIGHT: A view of* Queen Elizabeth´s *quarterdeck showing her massive 380mm (15in) guns and her observation balloon. The scale on the 380mm (15in) turret is for observing the turret's bearing.*

12
79
80   80
77
81   82   83
84   85   86
87   88   89
90
91
92

QUEEN ELIZABETH

*H*MS Queen Elizabeth *is widely regarded as a milestone in the history of the capital ship. She was the first to use oil as her sole fuel, and the first to be armed with 380mm (15in) guns. She underwent many changes in the course of a long life, and had at least one lucky escape from a premature demise. In the dark hours just before dawn, six days before Christmas 1941, three explosions rocked the British naval base of Alexandria. When the sky lightened, it was to reveal a scene of devastation – a tanker and two elderly battleships, HMSs* Valiant *and* Queen Elizabeth, *sister ships, rested on the bottom in shallow water, as a result of Operation GA 3, carried out by frogmen of the X Flottiglia MAS, led by Luigi Durand de la Penne.* Queen Elizabeth *was repaired in the USA, and is shown as she looked in June 1943.*

1. Captain
2. Wardroom
3. Commander
4. Officers' cabins
5. Wardroom pantry
6. Captain's pantry
7. Tiller room
8. Tiller head
9. Rudder
10. Screws
11. Bilge keel
12. 380mm (15in) gun (Mk I)
13. 0.5mm machine gun mount (Mk III)
14. Secondary command post
15. Secondary rangefinder (Mk IV)
16. Wireless aerial
17. Sound sensor
18. Searchlight
19. Boat boom
20. Ship's boat
21. Twin 114mm (4.4in) guns (Mk II and III)
22. Band room
23. Galley
24. Engineers' mess
25. Ventilator shaft to engine room
26. Engine room for catapult and crane
27. Wireless room
28. Auxiliary dynamo
29. Potato store
30. Pump room
31. Engine room for 114mm (4.4in) ammunition hoist
32. 114mm (4.4in) magazine
33. Engineers' pantry
34. Clothing store
35. Issuing office
36. Reduction gear
37. Turbines
38. Engine control room
39. Walrus scout plane
40. Crane for scout plane
41. Launch
42. Funnel uptakes
43. Ventilator shaft to boiler ro
44. Boiler room
45. Fuel tanks
46. Double bottom
47. Main rangefinder (Mk VII)
48. Bridge
49. Control centre
50. Chart room
51. Communications centre
52. Armoured access tube to
53. Sick bay
54. Dispensary
55. Ship's stores
56. Crew galley
57. Cold store
58. Refrigeration plant
59. Armoured belt
60. Wing passage
61. Plotting centre
62. Turret engine
63. Cable store
64. Upper shell handling room

FLASH

• HNLMS *De Ruyter* was 170.9 metres (560ft 6in) long overall with a beam of 15.7 metres (51ft 5in). She drew 5.1 metres (16ft 7in) at her full-load displacement of 6,961 tons, and her hull accounted for 2,650 tons, her machinery for 1,700 tons, her armour for 1,100 tons and her weapons for nearly 500 tons. The rotating part of each twin turret weighed over 70 tons.

• The new cruiser's keel was originally to have been laid on Friday 13 September 1933, but the operation was delayed a day for superstitious reasons.

• HNLMS *De Ruyter* had a full complement of 435 officers and men, and was equipped to serve as a flagship, with an additional admiral's suite and quarters for his staff.

• *De Ruyter* carried moored-mine minesweeping equipment in the shape of two paravanes attached to 55-metre (180ft) guide lines.

LEFT: With her five pairs of tri-axially stabilised 40mm (1.5in) Bofors anti-aircraft guns and advanced fire-control system for her 150mm (5.9in)/50 calibre main armament, De Ruyter was the one of the most advanced warships of her time. The picture clearly shows the single 150mm (5.9in) gun added to the design when it was decided to extend the ship.

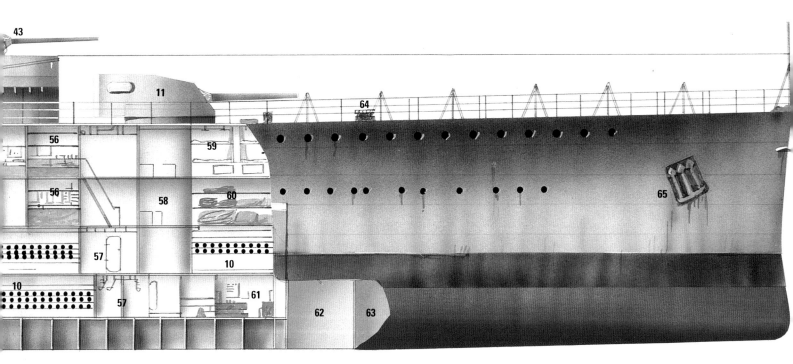

RIGHT: The view aft from the forecastle of Scharnhorst, down the barrels of the vessel's forward main armament. Hitler had it in mind to arm Scharnhorst and her sister with 380mm (14.9in) guns, but they were not available and so 280mm (11in) guns were installed instead. When Gneisenau was damaged by bombs in November 1942, plans were put in train to rebuild her with 380mm (14.9in) weapons, but she was never finished. Her main armament was removed for use in coastal batteries and she herself was sunk as a blockship at Gdynia in 1945.

LEFT: A post-rebuild picture of Scharnhorst with clipper bow in place. RIGHT: Since the Battle of the North Cape, in which Scharnhorst was sunk, took place in darkness, no photographs of any worth exist that show the battle itself. This picture shows survivors of the German commerce raider under guard on the catapult deck of the Royal Navy battleship Duke of York.

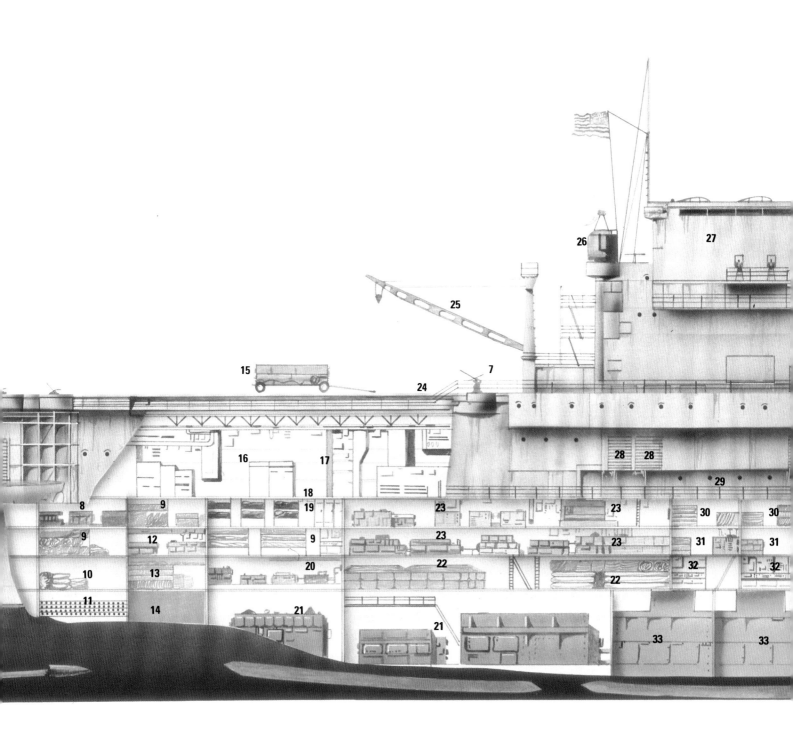

The flight deck of USS Enterprise *in April 1942. In the foreground are three-seater Douglas TBD-1 Devastator torpedo-bombers. The smaller aircraft are Grumman F4F-3 Wildcat fighters.*

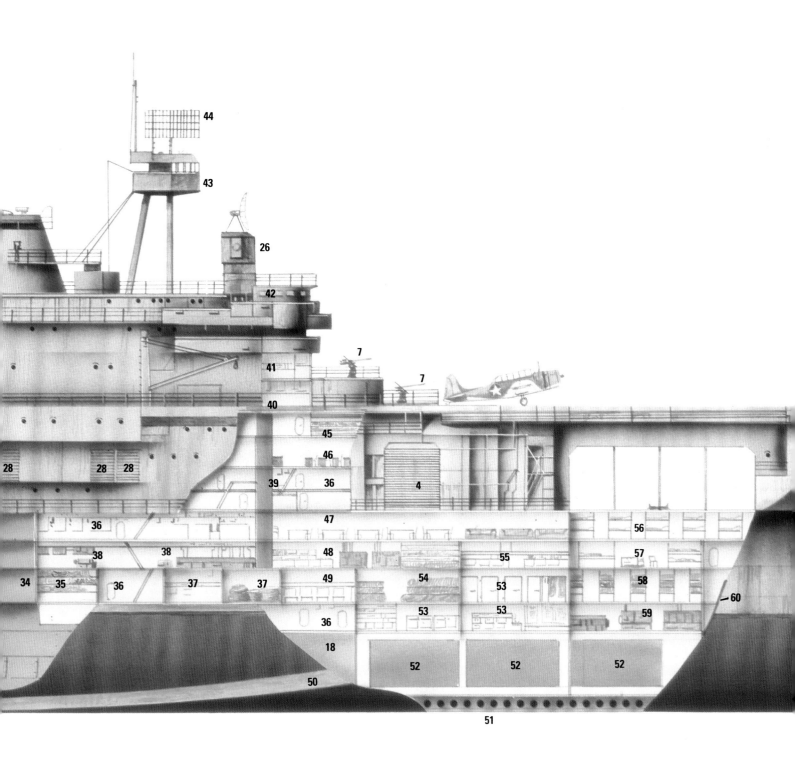

Guadalcanal landings, August 1942.
Ordnancemen of scouting squadron
6 load a 500-pound demolition bomb
on a Douglas SBD Dauntless dive-
bomber aboard USS Enterprise. *This*
picture was taken on 7 August, the
first day of the attacks on
Guadalcanal and Tulagi.

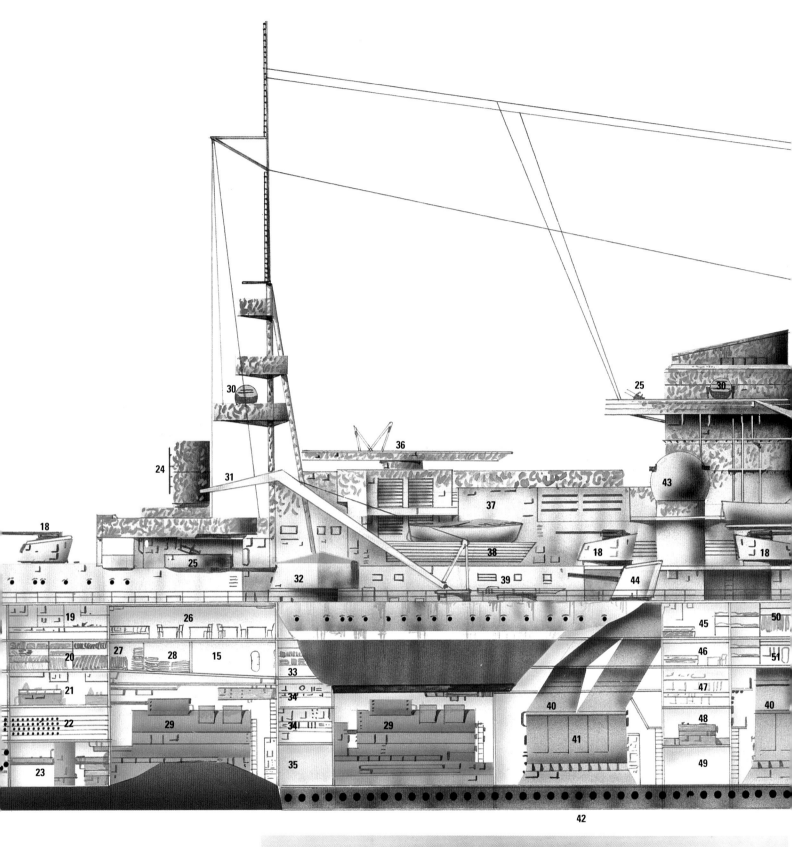

SCHARNHORST

Scharnhorst and Gneisenau, as eventually built, were intended by Hitler to give him powerful capital ships, but without provoking the British by trying too obviously to emulate their big-calibre battleships and battlecruisers in terms of armament. However, the ships had the reverse effect. They were eminently suited to the role of commerce raider, which worried the British. And their fears proved to be well founded when, during the first three months of 1941, in an operation codenamed 'Berlin', the two sisters, together with U boats, sank 22 merchant ships, totalling 114,175 tons, in the North Atlantic. Of that total, Scharnhorst alone accounted for almost 50,000 tons.

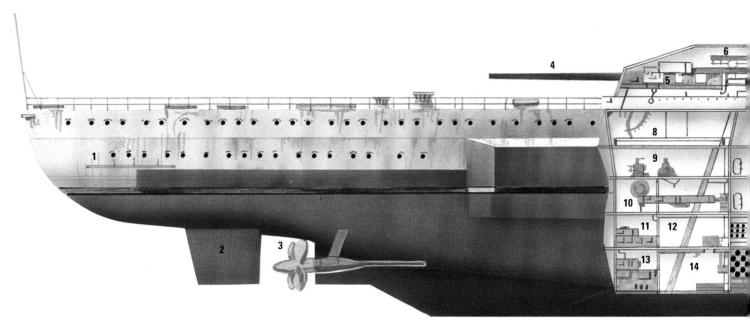

1. Fender rail	16. Secondary armament magazine	31. Main boat-handling crane
2. Rudder	17. Main magazine	32. 150mm (5.9in) guns in twin turrets
3. Screw	18. 105mm (4.1in) guns in twin mounts	33. Paint store
4. 280mm (11in) guns in triple turrets	19. Galley	34. Engineers' control centre
5. Gun cradle	20. Food store	35. Fresh water
6. Local rangefinder	21. Machine room	36. Seaplane launch catapult
7. Fume extractor	22. Anti-aircraft magazine	37. Seaplane hangar
8. Turntable	23. Auxiliary pump	38. Ventilators
9. Gun elevation machinery	24. Radar	39. 533mm (20.9in) torpedo tubes in triple mount
10. Hydraulic pump	25. 20mm (0.7in) anti-aircraft guns	40. Funnel uptake
11. Revolving cordite ring	26. Crew's mess	41. Boiler
12. Hoist	27. Potato store	42. Double bottom
13. Revolving shell ring	28. Cordage	43. Rangefinders for 150mm (5.9in) guns
14. Shell handling room	29. Engine	44. 150mm (5.9in) guns in single turrets
15. Companionway	30. Searchlight	45. Petty officers' quarters

FLASH

• *Enterprise*'s original air group in 1938 consisted of 18 fighters, 36 torpedo-bombers, 37 dive bombers, and five utility aircraft, a total of 96 aircraft. In the Battle of the Philippine Sea in June 1944 she carried 69 aircraft – 34 fighters (including three night fighters), 14 torpedo-bombers, and 21 dive bombers.

• *Enterprise*'s original armament consisted of 8 x 127mm (5in) guns in eight single turrets, 16 x 30mm (1.1in) machine guns in quadruple mounts, and 24 x 12.7mm (0.5in) machine guns in single mounts. At the end of the war, the 127mm (5in) armament was still there, but the remainder was made up of 11 quadruple 40mm (1.5in) mounts, eight twin 40mm (1.5in) mounts and 16 twin 20mm (0.7in) mounts.

• Once the first two Yorktown-class carriers had been ordered, only 15,000 tons (15,240 tonnes) remained of the USA's aircraft carrier tonnage under the terms of the Treaty of Washington. The decision was therefore made to build a single smaller carrier, which would form a class of her own. This ship was USS *Wasp*, commissioned in April 1940 and sunk in the Pacific in September 1942.

The dramatic scene on board Enterprise as firefighters wallow in the foam they are using to smother a deck fire caused by shrapnel from another ship. This incident took place towards the end of the war, by which time 'Big E' had been responsible for downing 911 enemy aircraft and her pilots had sunk 71 enemy ships.

ENTERPRISE

*T*he three Yorktown class ships were the first successful purpose-built American aircraft carriers, even though they were built to comply with the stringent terms of the Washington Naval Treaty of 1922. The treaty stipulated that the USA's carrier fleet was to be limited to 135,000 tons (137,160 tonnes) of new construction, and individual ships were not to exceed 27,000 tons (27,432 tonnes). Following the overweight Lexington-class ships, and Ranger, which had been launched in February 1933, just 55,000 tons (55,880 tonnes) of that total was left. This allowed the US Navy to build two Yorktown-class ships; Hornet *followed once treaty restrictions had been lifted.*

1. Rudder
2. Screws
3. 127mm (5in) 38 calibre guns
4. Hangar shutter
5. Side catapult
6. Boat crane
7. 30mm (1.1in) machine guns
8. Lift machinery
9. Ship's stores
10. Flood damage gear
11. Aviation magazine
12. Emergency dynamo
13. Engineers' stores
14. Fuel
15. Aviation fuel tanker
16. Hangar
17. Fire screen
18. 76mm (3in) armoured deck
19. Engineers' quarters
20. Machine shop
21. Engine room
22. Aviation stores
23. Aviation repair shop
24. Flight deck (wood-covered)
25. Crane (for loading supplies etc)
26. SC-type radar
27. Funnel casing
28. Air intakes
29. Side walkway
30. Petty officers' stores
31. Pump room
32. Engineers' control area
33. Boiler room
34. Funnel uptake
35. Clothes store
36. Wing passages
37. Cordage store
38. Electricians' department
39. Access tube to control centre
40. Flight deck control
41. Plotting centre
42. Bridge
43. Lookout station
44. CXAM-1 radar
45. Officers' stores
46. Briefing room
47. Crew rest area
48. Electricians' stores
49. Laundry
50. Bilge keel
51. Double bottom
52. Aviation fuel
53. Cold store
54. Food store
55. Galley
56. Crew
57. Sick bay
58. Tinned food store
59. Dynamo room
60. 102mm (4in)-thick armour belt

FLASH

• During trials, *Scharnhorst*'s three Brown Boveri geared turbines produced more power than the designers had expected, 161,764hp instead of 160,050 – allowing her three 4.45-metre (14ft 5in)-diameter propellers to drive her along at 31.65 knots.

• Much of *Scharnhorst*'s 32,480-ton unladen displacement was given over to armour, which made up 43.5 per cent of the total. The bare hull accounted for 25.5 per cent; the weapons and stores for them for 16.5 per cent; propulsion machinery for 8.9 per cent; and miscellaneous equipment for the remaining 5.6 per cent.

• *Scharnhorst* was divided into 21 watertight compartments and was double-bottomed for over three-quarters of her length. Thus when she was torpedoed below her C turret in June 1940 by the destroyer escort HMS *Acasta*, she made the safety of Trondheim, Norway, despite taking in 2,460 tons of water.

• In addition to her gun armament, *Scharnhorst* had six 533mm (20.9in) torpedo tubes. These had been removed from the light cruiser *Nürnberg*.

46. Engineers' mess
47. Boiler room control centre
48. Dynamo
49. Ballast tank
50. Crew's quarters
51. Engineers' quarters
52. Main rangefinders (280mm [11in] guns)
53. Navigation platform
54. Rangefinder for anti-aircraft guns
55. Upper bridge
56. Command centre
57. Local rangefinder housing
58. Breakwater
59. Ship's stores
60. Repair shop

61. Fuel
62. Barbette
63. 45mm (1.7in) inner armour skin
64. 350mm (13.7in) armour belt
65. 105mm (4.1in) armoured deck (sloping to sides)
66. Anchor
67. Decorative shield

53. Barbette
54. Medical centre
55. Crew
56. 380mm (14.9in) magazine
57. Loading tray for 380mm (14.9in) gun
58. Cradle for 380mm (14.9in) gun
59. Chase of 380mm (14.9in) gun
60. Turntable
61. Ammunition hoist
62. Loading room
63. Trim tanks
64. Fuel tanks

65. Turntable/elevation machinery
66. Auxiliary turntable machinery
67. 380mm (14.9in) reserve magazine
68. Crew messing area
69. Clothes issuing stores
70. Capstan machinery
71. Capstan
72. Boatswain's stores
73. Galley
74. Main anchor bed
75. Bow anchor

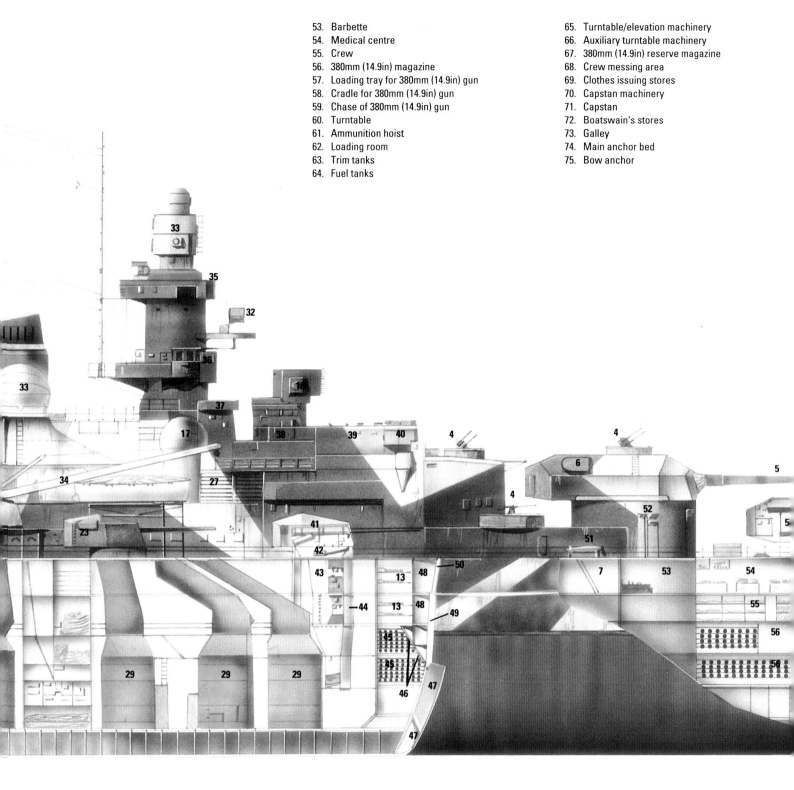

LEFT: Tirpitz in Narvik Bogen Fjord in July 1942, the month of the tragic Allied convoy PQ.17 to Russia. With the convoy under way, Tirpitz's berth at Trondheim, Norway, was found to be empty. Intelligence suggested that she was heading north, as were other German capital ships, presumably to attack the convoy on the night of 4 July. PQ.17 was ordered to disperse. The German capital ships were indeed gathering, but they did not sail until around noon on 5 July, by which time most of the scattered ships had fallen to U-boats and aircraft.

LEFT: The first Battle of Narvik, Norway, 10 April 1940. In broad daylight a force of five small British H-class destroyers entered Ofot Fjord, entrance to Narvik Harbour, where six more powerful German destroyers and a considerable fleet of supply ships lay. At dawn the next day the British ships steamed into the harbour in line ahead and commenced firing every gun and torpedo they had. They lost two of their number but sank six supply ships and a destroyer, and damaged three others. This picture shows the aftermath.

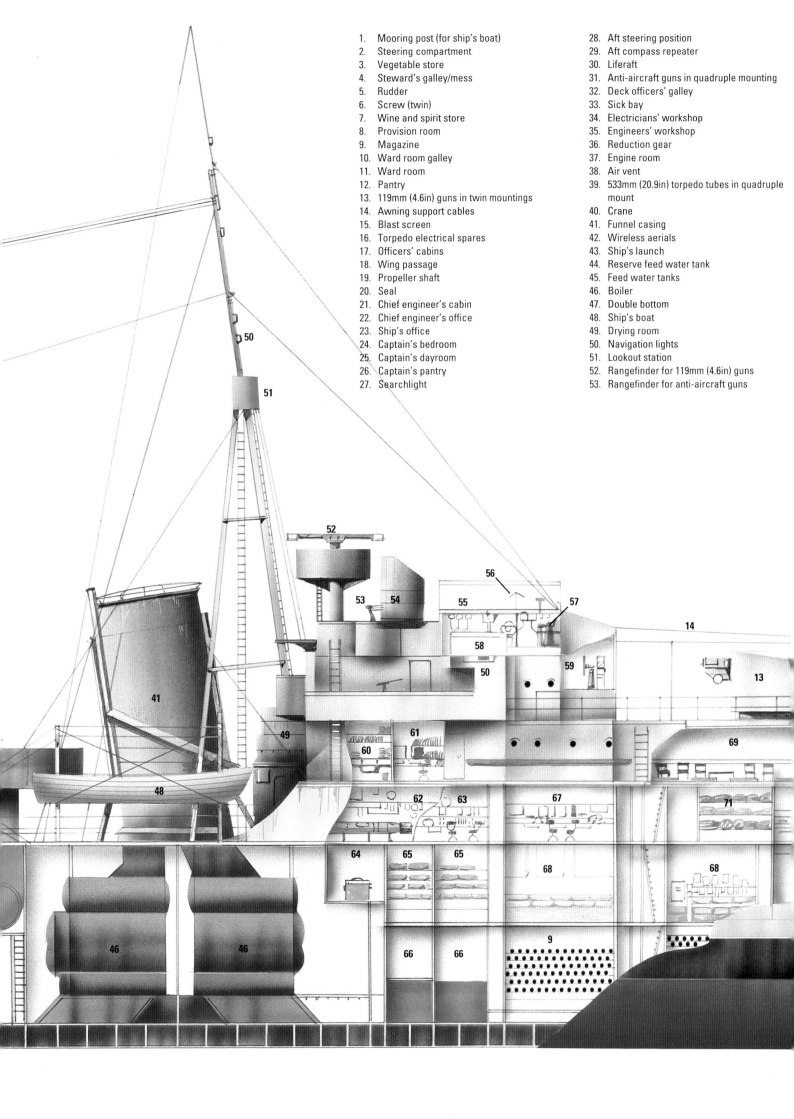

1. Mooring post (for ship's boat)
2. Steering compartment
3. Vegetable store
4. Steward's galley/mess
5. Rudder
6. Screw (twin)
7. Wine and spirit store
8. Provision room
9. Magazine
10. Ward room galley
11. Ward room
12. Pantry
13. 119mm (4.6in) guns in twin mountings
14. Awning support cables
15. Blast screen
16. Torpedo electrical spares
17. Officers' cabins
18. Wing passage
19. Propeller shaft
20. Seal
21. Chief engineer's cabin
22. Chief engineer's office
23. Ship's office
24. Captain's bedroom
25. Captain's dayroom
26. Captain's pantry
27. Searchlight
28. Aft steering position
29. Aft compass repeater
30. Liferaft
31. Anti-aircraft guns in quadruple mounting
32. Deck officers' galley
33. Sick bay
34. Electricians' workshop
35. Engineers' workshop
36. Reduction gear
37. Engine room
38. Air vent
39. 533mm (20.9in) torpedo tubes in quadruple mount
40. Crane
41. Funnel casing
42. Wireless aerials
43. Ship's launch
44. Reserve feed water tank
45. Feed water tanks
46. Boiler
47. Double bottom
48. Ship's boat
49. Drying room
50. Navigation lights
51. Lookout station
52. Rangefinder for 119mm (4.6in) guns
53. Rangefinder for anti-aircraft guns

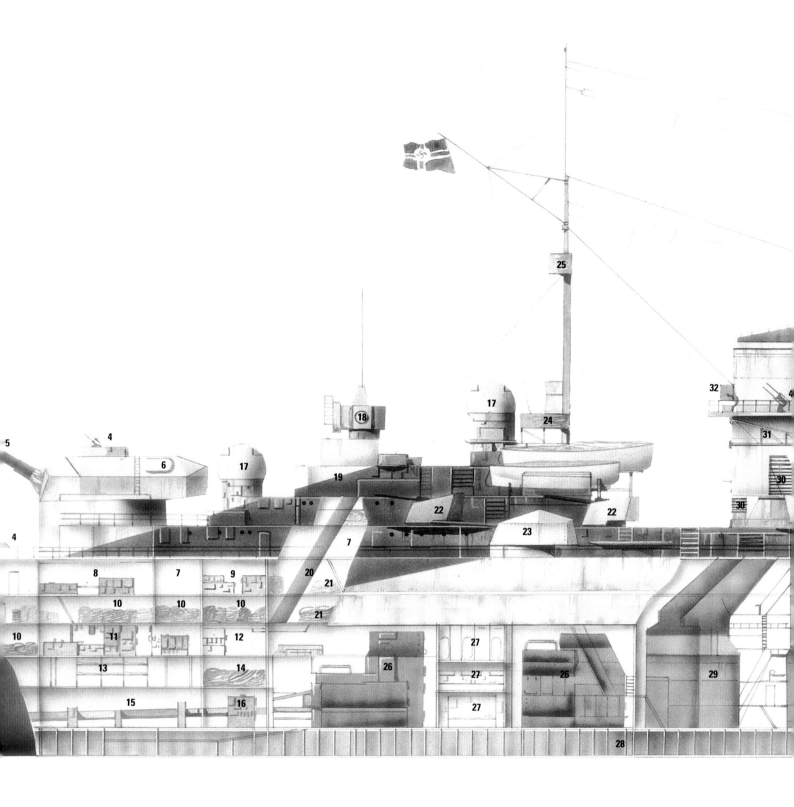

LEFT: This photograph of Tirpitz shows how camouflage was used to break up the ship's outline when she was berthed at Aas Fjord, Norway, in February 1942. Floating camouflage nets surround bow and stern, and netting has been draped between the port side of the vessel (the right-hand side in this picture) and the shore. The upper surface of the deck was also daubed with green paint in a random and irregular pattern to create the impression of a forest when seen from above.

TIRPITZ

*A*lthough she sortied only twice, and seldom fired anything larger than her many anti-aircraft guns in anger, Tirpitz, Hitler's biggest ship, played an important naval role during World War II, just by her very existence. The British considered her such a threat to her convoys to Russia that they poured vast resources into bringing about her destruction, and the ship effectively tied down a pair of Royal Navy capital ships, and often an aircraft carrier too, along with their respective screening forces.

1. Rudder	19. Aft control position	37. Admiral's bridge
2. Steering engine	20. Armoured access tube to control	38. Plotting room
3. Screws	21. Ship's stores	39. Main control centre
4. 20mm (0.7in) and 37mm (1.5in) anti-aircraft guns	22. Twin 102mm (4in) guns	40. Bridge
5. 380mm (14.9in) guns	23. Twin 150mm (5.9in) guns	41. Breech of 150mm (5.9in) gun
6. Sighting hood	24. Storage platform for lifeboats	42. Turntable of 150mm (5.9in) gun
7. Passage	25. Lookout post	43. Machinery for turning turret
8. Auxiliary dynamo room	26. Turbines	44. Armoured housing for turret machinery
9. Electricians' stores	27. Engine control centre	45. 150mm (5.9in) ammunition
10. Food storage	28. Double bottom	46. 100mm (3.9in)-thick sloping armoured deck
11. Dynamo	29. Boilers	47. Watertight compartments (partly used for fuel storage)
12. Cold store	30. Ventilators	48. Wing passages
13. Engineers' quarters	31. Small boat crane	49. 320mm (12.5in)-thick side armour
14. Engineers' stores	32. Searchlight	50. 270mm (10.6in)-thick side armour (reducing to 145mm (5.7in) at top)
15. Shaft	33. Rangefinder for main guns	51. Paravane sweep
16. Reduction gear	34. Main crane	52. Ventilation shaft to turret working areas
17. Rangefinder for secondary armament	35. Armoured upper (spotting) bridge	
18. Radar	36. Navigation bridge	

4. Director control (gunnery range and bearing)
5. Bridge
6. Semaphore
7. Captain's conning position
8. Chart table
9. Wheelhouse
10. Scullery
11. Second engineer's office
12. Torpedo room
13. Gunfire control office
14. Main compass room
15. Cordite store
16. Fuel tank
17. Transmitting station
18. Crew
19. Chief petty officer's mess
20. Hammock rack
21. Issue room (clothing etc)
22. Canteen
23. Potato room
24. Ammunition trunk
25. Breakwater
26. Windlass
27. Anchor

FLASH

THE COMING OF THE HEAVY DESTROYER

The Japanese were in the forefront of heavy destroyer development, bringing out in 1928 the first of the 20-ship Fubuki class, armed with six 125mm (4.9in) guns and nine 610mm (24in) torpedo tubes; the Fubukis were just short of 112 metres (370ft) long, had a trial displacement of 2,000 tons and a maximum speed of 38 knots. In the same year, the Italians unveiled the Navigatori class, with six 120mm (4.7in) guns and six 533mm (20.9in) torpedo tubes; they were shorter at 105 metres (344ft), but heavier at 2,578 tons full load, and shared the Fubukis' speed of 38 knots. France replied with the Le Fantasque class, which were almost light cruisers at 3,248 tons full load and almost 133 metres (436ft) overall, with five 138mm (5.4in) guns, and capable of maintaining 37 knots at full load. It wasn't until 1937 that the British launched the first of their 16 Tribals.

LEFT: The second Battle of Narvik, On 13 April 1940, a British flotilla led by the battleship Warspite and including Cossack and three other Tribals came back to Narvik. A matter of hours later, every German warship and supply ship had been accounted for, all the shore batteries had been destroyed and the important iron-ore port had been rendered unusable for nine months.

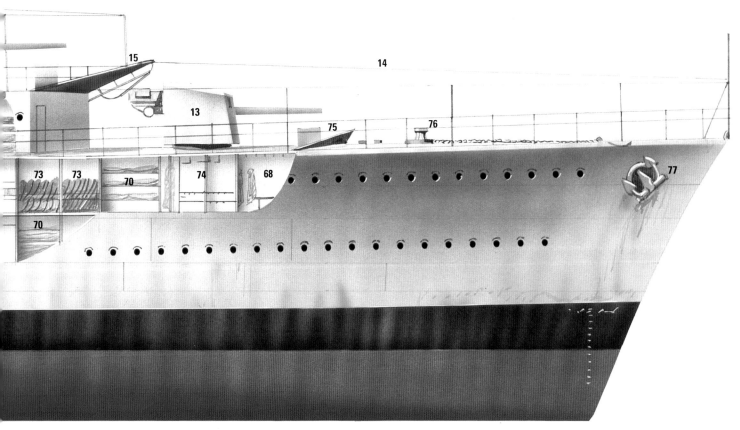

COSSACK

*I*n the period between the two World Wars, the navies of the Great
Powers were limited by the Washington Treaty in the number and size
of the biggest ships they could build. One of the areas naval architects
concentrated on instead was the development of the destroyer, which had
grown during World War I from an 80-metre-long (262ft) ship of about
985 tons to average around 100 metres (328ft) overall, with a deep-load
displacement of 1,476 tons. These ships mounted four to six guns of up to
about 100mm (3.9in), the same number of torpedo tubes, and were
capable of around 35 knots. Over the next 20 years, the ships almost
doubled in displacement and grew to an overall length of around 115
metres (377ft), all the increase going to support a much heavier weapons
load. The Japanese, French and Italians all developed these heavy
destroyers; Cossack *and the Tribals were Britain's answer to them.*

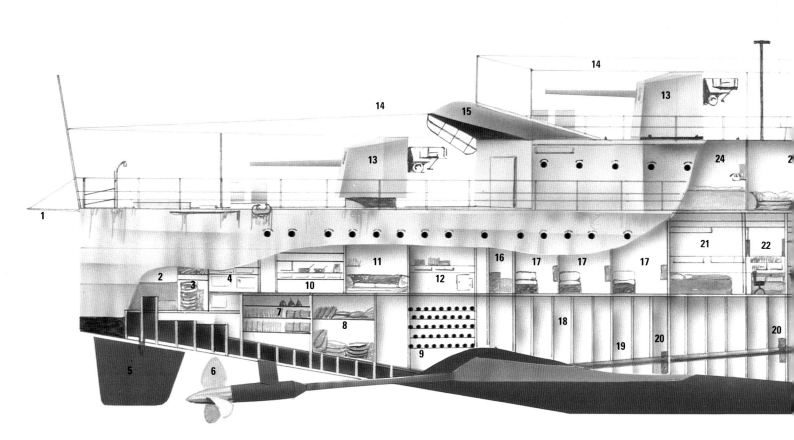

FLASH

• *Tirpitz* was powered by three-shaft Brown-Boveri geared turbines fed by 12 Wagner boilers. These delivered 138,000 shaft horsepower, enough for a top speed of 29 knots. At a cruising speed of 19 knots, she had a range of 16,650 kilometres (8,763 nautical miles).

• *Tirpitz* and her sister carried a main armament of eight 380mm (14.9in) guns in four twin turrets. The French, whom Hitler perceived as the main threat to Germany when he laid down *Tirpitz* and *Bismarck*, were building the *Richelieu* and *Jean Bart* with eight 381mm (15in) guns in four twins; the Italians the Littorio class ships with nine similar-sized weapons in three triples. In Europe, only the Royal Navy's unusual-looking *Nelson* and *Rodney* had substantially bigger (9 x 406mm [15.9in]) guns, whereas the two biggest Japanese battleships, *Yamato* and *Musashi*, by far the largest such ships ever, comfortably outgunned everything in the world with their nine 460mm (18in) rifles.

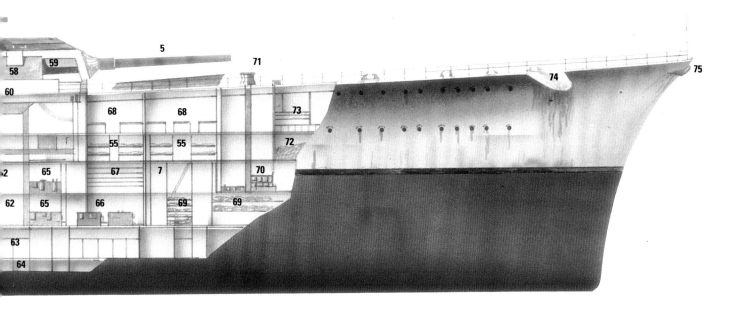

LEFT: In a fjord somewhere in Norway dancers entertain the crew of the Tirpitz. Tirpitz *was stationed in Norwegian waters from January 1942 until she was capsized and put out of action for good by RAF Lancasters in November 1944. Note the camouflage on the 380mm (14.9in) guns, which were fired in anger only once, during the bombardment of Spitsbergen in September 1943.*

32

33

34

25

35

36

31

30

29

29

3

37

40

43

44

45

45

38

39 39 39 39

41

42

ABOVE: The other main type of US PT boat in World War II
was the 78-foot Higgins model. This photograph was taken
in 1944 and shows the PT463 travelling at speed. She

LEFT: Yamato *fitting out at Kure, Japan on 9 September 1941. Not until after Pearl Harbor did US naval intelligence get wind of her true size and power. The old aircraft carrier* Hosho *can just be seen on the extreme right of the picture.*

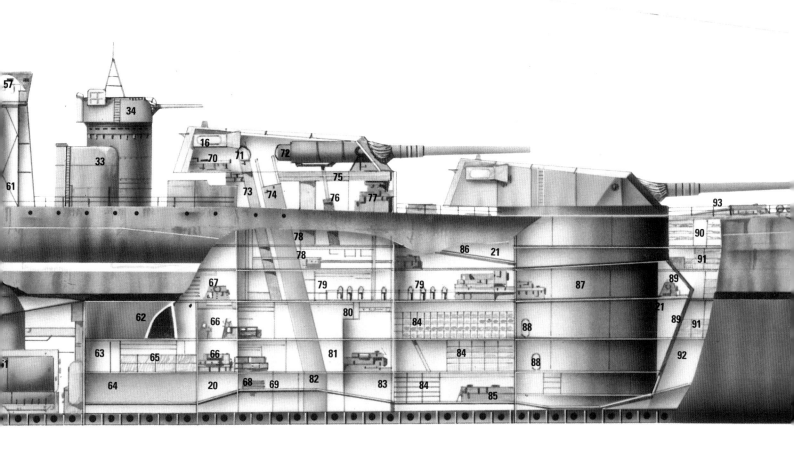

1. Navigation lights
2. Crane
3. Catapult
4. Catapult machinery
5. Armoured area for rudder head
6. Rudder machinery
7. Impulse motor for steering control
8. Rudder
9. Propeller
10. Armoured control area for
    secondary rudders
11. Floatplane (for scouting)
12. Aviation stores
13. Air crew quarters
14. Propeller shaft
15. 460mm (18in) gun
16. Range finder
17. Double bottom
18. Dynamo

19. Bilge pump
20. Spare storage/Emergency buoyancy
21. Aft armoured bulkhead (300mm
    (11.8in) thick)
22. Ship's stores
23. Artillery stores
24. Aft damage control
25. Office
26. Shell room
27. Ventilation plant
28. Crew quarters
29. Fuel pump room
30. Cordite racks
31. Fuel tank
32. Top of armoured belt
33. Ventilator intake trunk
34. 155mm (6.1in) 55 calibre gun turret
35. Local range finder
36. 25mm (0.9in) anti-aircraft guns (four

per mounting)
37. Armoured aft control centre
38. Aft range finder
39. Wireless antenna
40. Twin 127mm (5in) 40 calibre guns
41. Searchlight
42. Control centre for searchlights
43. Funnel
44. Superheaters
45. Armoured cover to funnel uptakes
46. Funnel uptakes
47. 200-300mm (7.8-11.8in) armour deck
48. Turbine room
49. No. 3 boiler room
50. No. 2 boiler room
51. No. 1 boiler room
52. Secondary rangefinder
53. Main rangefinder for 460mm (18in)
    guns

ABOVE: John F. Kennedy, the future President of the USA, during his service as a PT-boat officer in the Pacific during World War II. He was commander of the PT109 on the night of 1/2 August 1943, when it was rammed and sliced in two by the Japanese destroyer Amagiri.

ABOVE: The 80-foot Elco boats were often given striped dazzle paintwork as camouflage. This boat is an early model of the 80-foot class, like the PT109, with twin machine guns mounted in turrets.

PT109

*A*s originally conceived, the 80-foot Elco was a hard-chine hull, 24.4 metres (80ft) in length, with a beam of 6.3 metres (20ft), a draught of just 1.7 metres (5ft 5in) at rest and a displacement of just under 55 tons when fully loaded. It was fitted with three Packard 4M2500 V-12 supercharged petrol engines, which were initially rated at 1,350hp, but which were developing over 1,500hp by the end of World War II. They gave the boat a theoretical top speed of over 40 knots, though that was soon reduced in practice by fouling, and by water being absorbed by the hull. Later boats, which had Mk 13 torpedoes in roll-off racks fitted in place of launch tubes, were probably a little faster, at least when new.

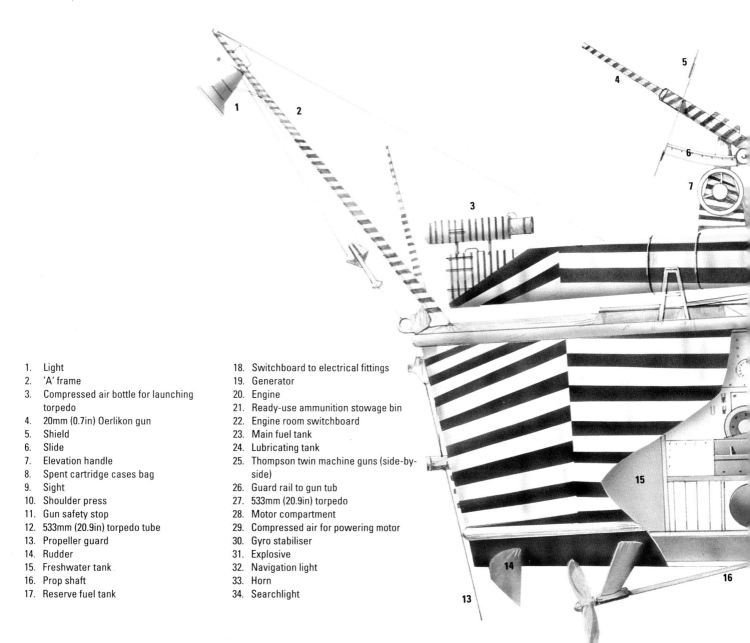

1. Light
2. 'A' frame
3. Compressed air bottle for launching torpedo
4. 20mm (0.7in) Oerlikon gun
5. Shield
6. Slide
7. Elevation handle
8. Spent cartridge cases bag
9. Sight
10. Shoulder press
11. Gun safety stop
12. 533mm (20.9in) torpedo tube
13. Propeller guard
14. Rudder
15. Freshwater tank
16. Prop shaft
17. Reserve fuel tank
18. Switchboard to electrical fittings
19. Generator
20. Engine
21. Ready-use ammunition stowage bin
22. Engine room switchboard
23. Main fuel tank
24. Lubricating tank
25. Thompson twin machine guns (side-by-side)
26. Guard rail to gun tub
27. 533mm (20.9in) torpedo
28. Motor compartment
29. Compressed air for powering motor
30. Gyro stabiliser
31. Explosive
32. Navigation light
33. Horn
34. Searchlight

FLASH

• *Yamato* had an overall length of 263m (862ft), a beam of 36.9m (121ft) and a draught of 10.4m (34ft). She had a standard displacement of 63,315 tons and a full-load displacement of 69,990 tons.

• In addition to *Yamato* and her three sisters, three further huge battleships were considered, including two – the unnamed Nos. 798 and 799 – with 508mm (20in) main armament.

• It took between ten and 19 torpedoes plus 17 bombs to sink *Musashi* during the Battle of Leyte Gulf in 1944; *Yamato* succumbed to between nine and 13 torpedoes and six bombs on 7 April 1945.

• Each of *Yamato*'s gun turrets weighed 2,530 tons, and the guns, at a 45-degree elevation, could hurl a 1,460kg (3,212lb) armour-piercing projectile more than 42,000 metres (45,931 yards).

54. Rangefinder for anti-aircraft guns
55. Navigation bridge
56. Rangefinder for anti-aircraft and secondary guns
57. Main control centre
58. Armoured access tube to main rangefinder
59. Main damage control centre
60. Emergency medical centre
61. Armoured tube (300mm/11.8in) to main control centre
62. Hull bulge (double hull for defence against torpedoes)
63. Access to boiler rooms
64. Feed water tank to boilers
65. Machine room stores
66. Machine room
67. Emergency engine for controlling turret

68. Emergency bilge pump
69. 50-80mm (1.9-3.1in) thick floor to turret base
70. Shell carriage and rammer
71. Tilting shell bucket
72. Breech of 460mm (18in) gun
73. Shell hoist
74. Cordite cage trunk
75. Gun carriage
76. Elevation cylinder
77. Elevation control engine
78. Shell handling rooms
79. Lower shell handling room
80. Flashtight scuttle
81. Lower cordite handling room
82. Central pivot to turret
83. 50mm thick armour inner wall
84. Cordite room
85. Electrical machine shop

86. 230mm (9in) thick armour deck to magazine and working area
87. Barbette tower
88. Flashtight entry doors
89. 300mm (11.8in) thick armoured bulkhead
90. Crew sleeping and mess area
91. Food store
92. Forward trim tank
93. Breakwater
94. Anchor crane/Loading crane
95. Winch
96. Anchor cable
97. Anchor
98. Secondary anchor port
99. Prow
100. Bow bulb

YAMATO

*T*he construction of Yamato *and her sister ships caused great
technical problems, and the design was recast many times.*
Yamato *entered service with nine 460mm (18in) guns, twelve
155mm (6.1in)guns and twelve 127mm (5in) guns plus anti-aircraft
armament; in 1943 six of the 155mm (6.1in) weapons were replaced
with a further twelve 127mm (5in) guns, and the AA defence was
regularly upgraded. Though there can be no doubt that the Yamatos
were immensely powerful ships, the money, manpower and materials
consumed could have been put to better use building a balanced fleet.
The illustration shows* Yamato *as she would have looked in 1942.*

FLASH

• In the late 1930s, Elco approached the British Power Boat Company and purchased an example and the plans of a revolutionary 70-foot boat that the British company had developed at its own expense. With some local modification, this design became the 70-foot Elco, which served in the US Navy as *PT10-19* and in anti-submarine form as *PTC1-12*. All 23 boats were eventually transferred to the Royal Navy.

• Elco were not the only PT boat manufacturers in the USA. Higgins of New Orleans developed their 78-foot PT, which became the other major US World War II type, and there were a small number of Huckins types that were generally used for training. A large number of British 73-foot Vosper types were also built in the USA and transferred to the Royal Navy and the Soviet Union under Lend-Lease, along with a number of Elco and Higgins boats.

• PT boats fought most of their actions in the Pacific, but in the lead-up to the D-Day landings of June 1944, a force of PTs arrived in Europe. They were brought in for covert operations, but during the landings they combined with Allied fast attack craft to protect the invasion fleet from their German equivalents – the S-boats.

rpedoes: by this date PT boats were often s gunboats than torpedo boats.

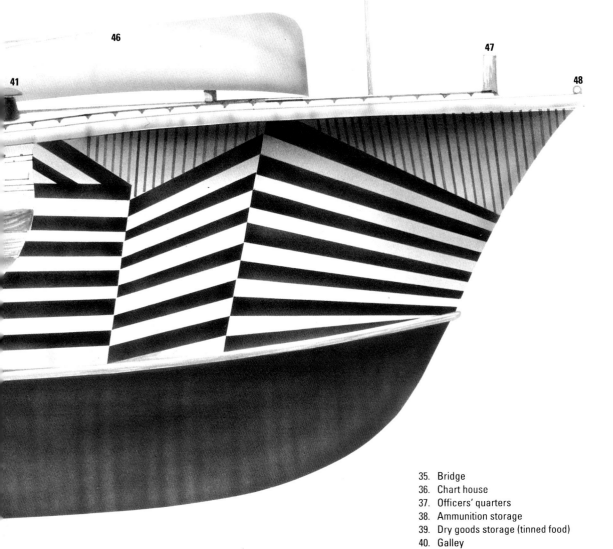

35. Bridge
36. Chart house
37. Officers' quarters
38. Ammunition storage
39. Dry goods storage (tinned food)
40. Galley
41. Mushroom-shaped ventilator
42. Footrail
43. Crew's quarters
44. Mess
45. Ship's stores
46. Dinghy (when carried)
47. Mooring bit
48. Fairlead

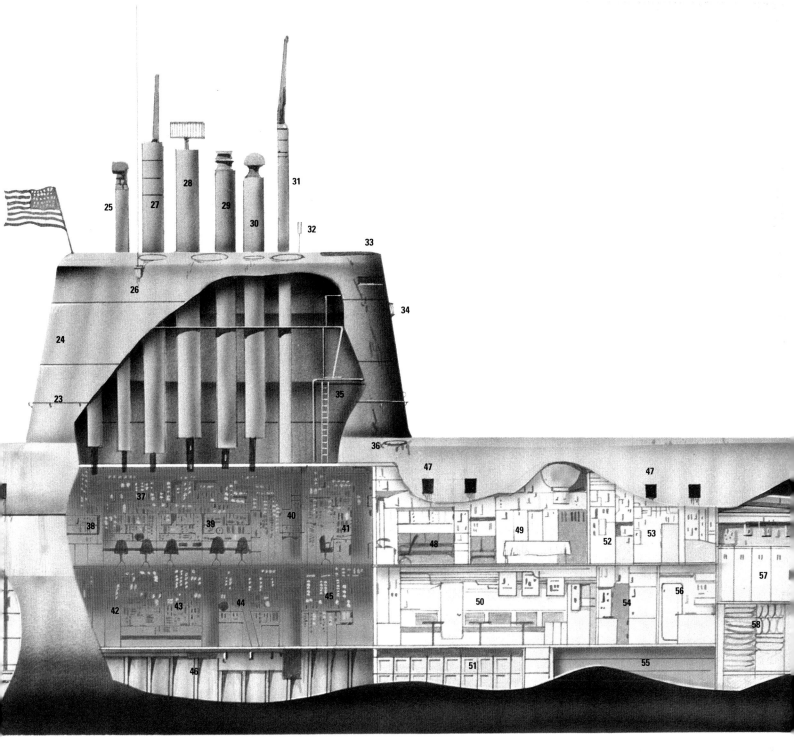

25 26 27 28 29 30 31 32 33 34 23 24 35 36 37 38 39 40 41 42 43 44 45 46 47 48 49 50 51 52 53 54 55 56 57 58

LEFT: A US Navy lieutenant looks through Nautilus' *periscope.* Nautilus' *depth limit was stated as in excess of 120m (390ft), but she may have been able to go as deep as 220m (720ft). RIGHT:* Nautilus *after she had collided with the US aircraft carrier* Essex *in November 1966.* Nautilus *was travelling not far beneath the surface when the incident occurred and was damaged, but there were no reports of any casualties.*

1. Fantail
2. AA sponson
3. Crane
4. Curtiss SCI Seahawk float plane
5. Catapult
6. Turning gear/Compressed air stowage
7. Air service stores
8. Aviation fuel
9. Air crew quarters
10. Air maintenance
11. Rudder
12. Quadruple screws
13. 20mm (0.7in) AA battery
14. 406mm (15.9in), 50 calibre main armament
15. Sight for local control of main armament
16. 40mm (1.5in) AA guns
17. Optical director for main guns and 127mm (5in) guns
18. Fire control radar, main guns
19. Fire control radar, AA weapons
20. Outer search radar
21. Optical workshop (used to maintain sights)
22. Galley
23. Fresh food store
24. Wing passage
25. Crew/Stokers
26. Funnel uptakes
27. Mess attendants/Galley
28. Radar room
29. 40mm (1.5in) ready ammunition store
30. Showers
31. Officers' wardroom

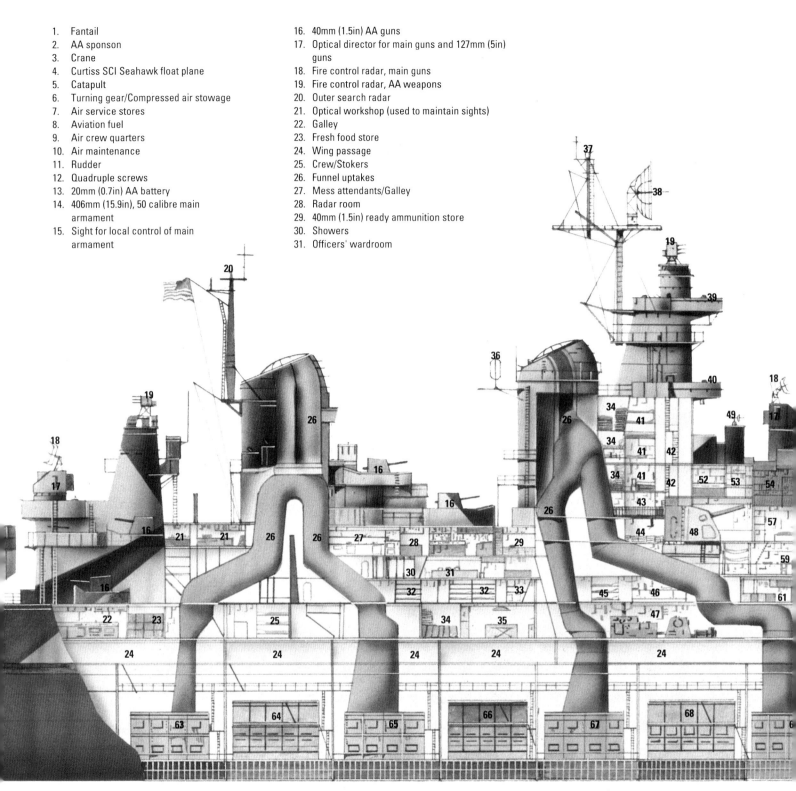

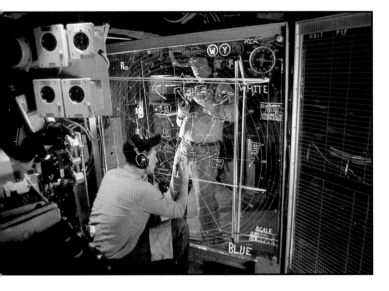

LEFT: Crewmen at work in Iowa's Combat Engagement Center during December 1984. The installation of a Combat Engagement Center was part of the reactivation refit package and is where sensor information is processed to enable the ship to keep track of friendly and hostile movements.

32. Crew spaces
33. Master at arms
34. Stores
35. Main surgery (theatre)
36. Wireless loop
37. Sky search radar
38. Main search radar
39. Lookout station
40. Ship conning bridge
41. Officers' quarters
42. Armoured access tube to upper bridges
43. Stowage for 127mm (5in) ammunition
44. Repair station
45. Mess attendants' quarters
46. Auxiliary control centre
47. Electric shop
48. 127mm (5in) dual-purpose gun
49. AA fire control
50. Searchlight platform
51. Upper bridge
52. Compass room
53. Wireless room
54. Flag plot, navigation
55. Bridge

56. Armoured conning tower bridge
57. Captain's quarters
58. Control centre
59. Operations office
60. Landing force equipment
61. Main radio control room
62. Machine room
63. No. 4 Boiler room
64. No. 3 Engine room
65. No. 3 Boiler room
66. No. 2 Engine room
67. No. 2 Boiler room
68. No. 1 Engine room
69. No. 1 Boiler room
70. Small arms/powder room
71. Dynamo
72. Double bottom, used for fuel storage
73. Shell room for 406mm (15.9in) guns
74. Access flap to loading bay
75. Centre loading area
76. Gun turret rotating drive
77. Ready-to-use stowage
78. Local sightfinders position, used if main directors out of action

79. Slide and rammer
80. Shell hoist
81. Counter recoil
82. Turret roller
83. Roller path
84. Training buffer
85. Gun slide/seat
86. Powder hoist
87. Lower shell hoist (split in case of fire in upper compartment)
88. Loading bay to hoist
89. Marines
90. Plotting room to main guns
91. Ship's stores/Ordnance stores
92. Barbette
93. Main armour belt
94. Sick bay
95. Main supply department stores
96. Chief petty officers' mess area
97. Paravane for clearing mines
98. Local control to 44mm (1.7in) guns
99. Anchor
100. Hawser

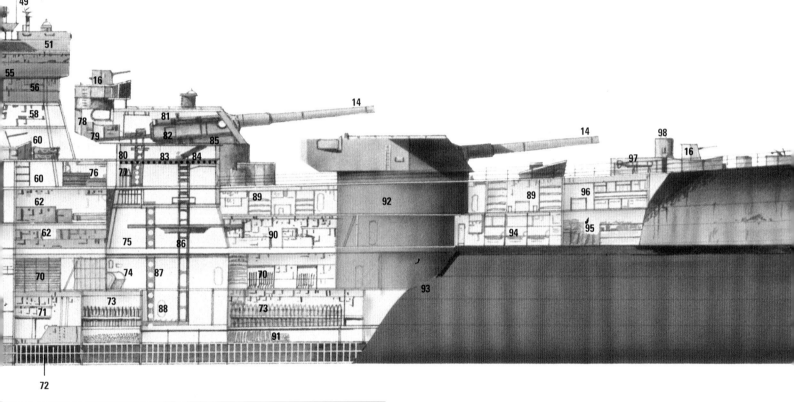

LEFT: Each 406mm (15.9in) turret is manned by a crew of 77, backed up by another 30-36 men working in the magazine. Between them they can ensure a rate of fire of two rounds per minute. The barrels and ammunition for the 406mm (15.9in) armament are no longer manufactured and the guns must now rely on what is left in storage. In 1986, this was believed to be around 34 spare barrels and more than 20,000 rounds of ammunition.

1. Tail
2. Screw
3. Drive shaft
4. Outer casing
5. Aft crew quarters
6. Aft feed pump
7. Compressed air
8. Escape trunk
9. Engine control room
10. Reduction gear
11. Main engine room
12. Sea water service pump
13. Steam turbine
14. Turbo generator
15. Diesel generator
16. Motor room
17. Gearbox
18. Circulation pump
19. Electric motor
20. Bypass pump
21. Reactor
22. Turbo feed pumps
23. Handrail

24. Fin (conning tower)
25. Direction finding antenna
26. Radio
27. General purpose periscope
28. Radar
29. Multi-purpose antenna
30. Snorkel
31. Attack periscope
32. Identity beacon
33. Bridge
34. Navigation light
35. Trunk to bridge
36. Maintenance hatch
37. Attack centre
38. Fore engine room control
39. Attack control
40. Periscope
41. Radar
42. Sonar
43. Navigation room
44. Back up attack centre
45. Torpedo control centre
46. Main ballast tank

47. Drain
48. Captain's cabin
49. Officers' wardroom
50. Crew messdeck
51. Batteries
52. Galley
53. Cold store
54. Crew galley
55. Fresh water tank
56. Officers' store/office
57. Crew's quarters
58. Stores
59. Tethered marker buoy with telephone
60. Torpedo room
61. Torpedo reloads
62. Torpedo tubes
63. Inner hull
64. Anchor well
65. Bow planes
66. Sonar access point
67. Torpedo exit ports

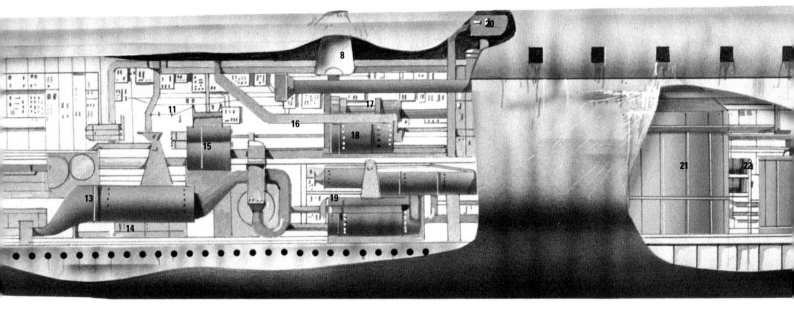

LEFT: Nautilus *is welcomed as she arrives in New York City.* *RIGHT:* *A crewman at the controls of* Nautilus. Nautilus *was the first nuclear-powered vessel. Her pressurised water-cooled reactor was linked to steam turbines, forming a powerplant capable of generating 15,000 shaft horsepower. This gave her a surface speed of over 20 knots and a submerged speed of over 22.5 knots.*

NAUTILUS

USS Nautilus *was, at the time of her commissioning, by far the largest submarine in the world. She had a length of 97 metres (318ft), a beam of 8.2 metres (26ft 9in) and a surface displacement of 4,091 tons; her complement was 11 officers and 100 enlisted men. Her hull was based on the German Type XXI U-boat of late World War II, even though the USA had already developed the potentially faster and more manoeuvrable 'tear-drop' hull.*

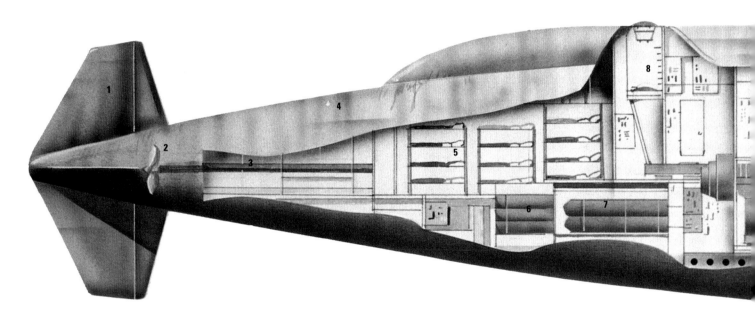

RIGHT: Commander William R. Anderson USN, commanding officer of the USS Nautilus, *climbs the gangplank from the submarine after she has docked at Portland, England following her epoch-making cruise beneath the polar ice. In fact, once* Nautilus *had emerged beyond the pole, Commander Anderson had been airlifted off in mid-ocean to report personally to the US President. He rejoined his ship as she was approaching Portland.*

FLASH

- The complement of an Iowa-class ship is 1,518 – 65 officers and 1,453 men.

- The cost of constructing *Iowa* was officially stated to be more than $100 million. The cost of refitting her for reactivation in the 1980s was $405 million – less than the price of one Oliver Hazard Perry class frigate.

- Iowa class ships are extremely well protected by today's standards – each has a 305mm (12in) armour belt, 345mm (13.5in) armour on the propeller shafts, 432mm (17in) armour on the turret faces, 184mm (7.2in) on the tops, and 305mm (12in) on the backs.

- Apart from the Japanese pair *Yamato* and *Musashi*, the Iowas were the largest battleships ever built.

- In addition to a multitude of shipborne sensors, Iowas are equipped with five remotely piloted vehicles (RPV) for recce and targeting.

LEFT: Pallets of 406mm (15.9in) ammunition awaiting transfer to the magazines. The main armament can fire two types of shell – a 862kg (1,900lb) high-explosive (HE) round and a 1,225kg (2,700lb) armour-piercing (AP) round. A tactical nuclear shell was also developed for these guns during the 1950s. Designated the Mk 23 'Kate', it carried a W23 warhead and remained on the nuclear stockpile until October 1962. Iowa-class battleships were to carry ten of these shells, although it is believed that none were ever taken to sea.

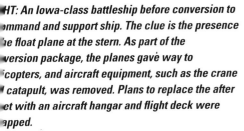

HT: An Iowa-class battleship before conversion to [co]mmand and support ship. The clue is the presence [of th]e float plane at the stern. As part of the [con]version package, the planes gave way to [heli]copters, and aircraft equipment, such as the crane [and] catapult, was removed. Plans to replace the after [turr]et with an aircraft hangar and flight deck were [scr]apped.

IOWA

*T*he Iowa-class battleships were a departure from usual US practice – instead of sacrificing speed to heavy armament and armour protection, they were fast, heavily armed and well protected at the same time. But they were built for a purpose – to form part of fast aircraft carrier task forces which would be pitted against similar Japanese carrier groups in the Pacific. Iowa *is shown here as she would have looked at the end of World War II.*

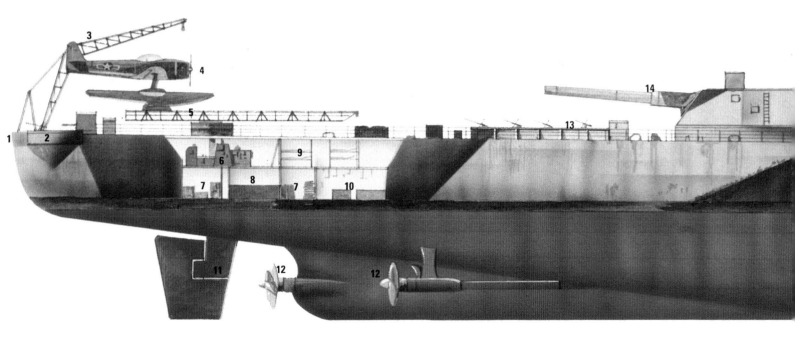

LEFT: Iowa *being moved on 22 April 1982 in preparation for her refit before reactivation as a command and support ship. This refit included the installation of BGM-109 Tomahawk cruise missile launchers (which replaced four of the ten 127mm [5in] mountings), RGM-84 Harpoon anti-ship missile launchers, plus improvements to her electronics. She was recommissioned in April 1984.*

FLASH

- *Nautilus* cost $40 million to build, of which $25 million was spent on the nuclear reactor.

- Admiral Hyman Rickover (1900-86), who masterminded the *Nautilus* project, was still serving in the US Navy in 1981, a year after *Nautilus* herself had retired. He was by then the Navy's oldest and longest-serving admiral.

- Power from the *Nautilus'* nuclear reactor was used to begin welding on the keel of the Polaris submarine *USS Lafayette*, when she was laid down on 17 January 1961, the sixth anniversary of *Nautilus'* first trip under nuclear power.

- On 3 May 1980, *Nautilus* was defuelled and decommissioned at Mare Island, California. She was later towed to Groton, Connecticut, where she took up station as a museum on 6 July 1985.

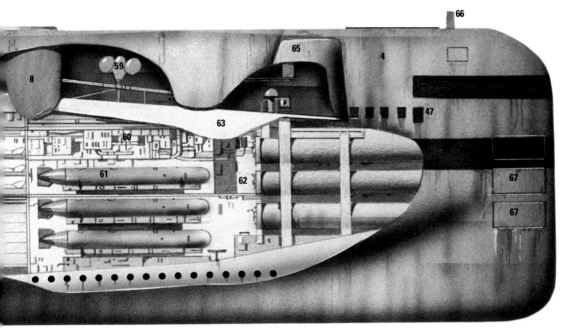

RIGHT: The torpedo room of Nautilus *as she passes under the polar ice pack in 1958. The tubes were kept ready in case she needed to blast her way out of trouble. Despite her reputation as a record-breaker,* Nautilus *was first and foremost an attack submarine and carried six 533mm (20.9in) torpedo tubes, all mounted in the bow. She also carried the powerful and accurate BQS-4 and BQS-2C sonar sets.*

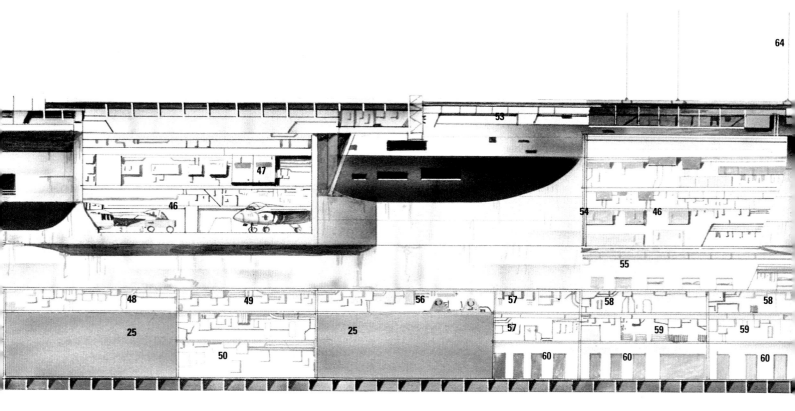

53

47

46

54 46

55

48 49 56 57 58 58

25 25 57 59 59

50 60 60 60

-coded

s a
j
ereas
nge
n hit

:
v.

ABOVE: Writing backwards, a crewman makes an entry on the screen in the flight deck control center.

RIGHT: A look up at the forest of masts atop the island of the Dwight D. Eisenhower. *Nimitz-class carriers are equipped with a battery of radars, including an SPS-49 long-range air-search radar, with a range of 457km (240 nautical miles), and an SPS-48 height-finder radar with a range of 402km (212 nautical miles). These carriers also carry radar sets for surface search, navigation, and aircraft landing; and radars are also used in conjunction with the surface-to-air missile fire control system.*

RIGHT: A photograph of Long Beach *taken in January 1962. It shows the Talos long-range surface-to-air missile launchers mounted on the vessel's stern. The Talos system was replaced in 1979 with two quadruple Harpoon anti-ship missile launchers.*
FAR RIGHT: *Long Beach* (CGN9, right) *at sea in the Arabian Gulf. She is accompanied by USS* Bunker Hill (CG52), *a Ticonderoga class guided missile escort cruiser.*

23. Turret turning motor
24. Shell hoist
25. Control centre for 127mm (5in) weapons
26. Shell room
27. Radar/Fire-control tower for 127mm (5in) guns
28. Derrick
29. Anti-submarine rocket launcher
30. Damage control centre
31. Auxiliary pump room
32. Lubricating oil tanks

33. Officers' mess
34. Heat exchanger
35. Nuclear reactor
36. Generator room
37. Admiral's/Captain's quarters
38. Command centre
39. Radar command centre
40. Armour plating
41. Navigation centre
42. Bridge
43. Admiral's plotting centre
44. Elevator

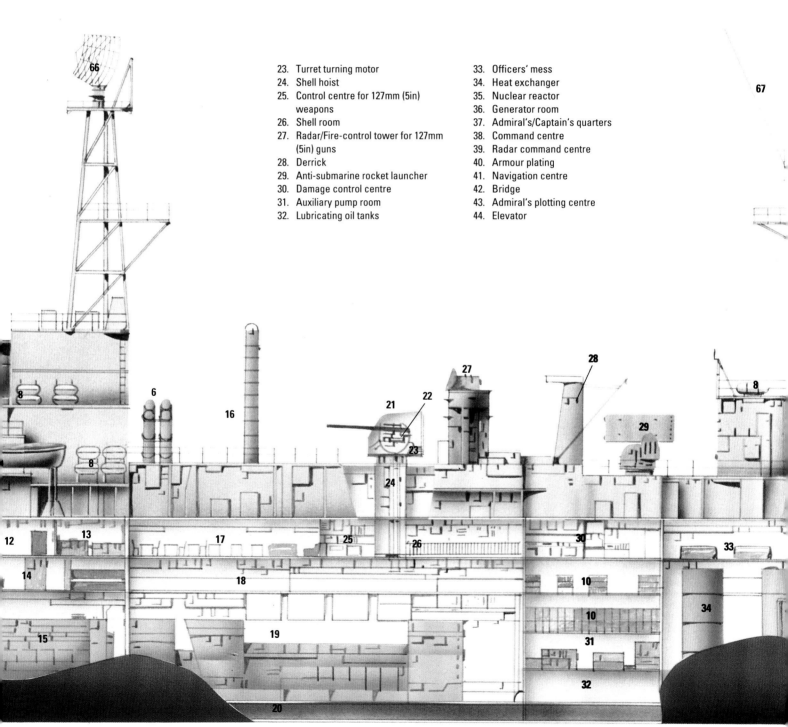

ABOVE: Long Beach *(left) in the company of the Wichita-class replenishment vessel* Kansas City *(AOR3, centre). On the right is the Spruance-class destroyer* Leftwich *(DD984).*

69

70

71

72

72

40

41

39

42

43

38

44

37

72

72

55

54

53

56

45

50

50

50

57

49

46

35

51

47

34

52

48

48

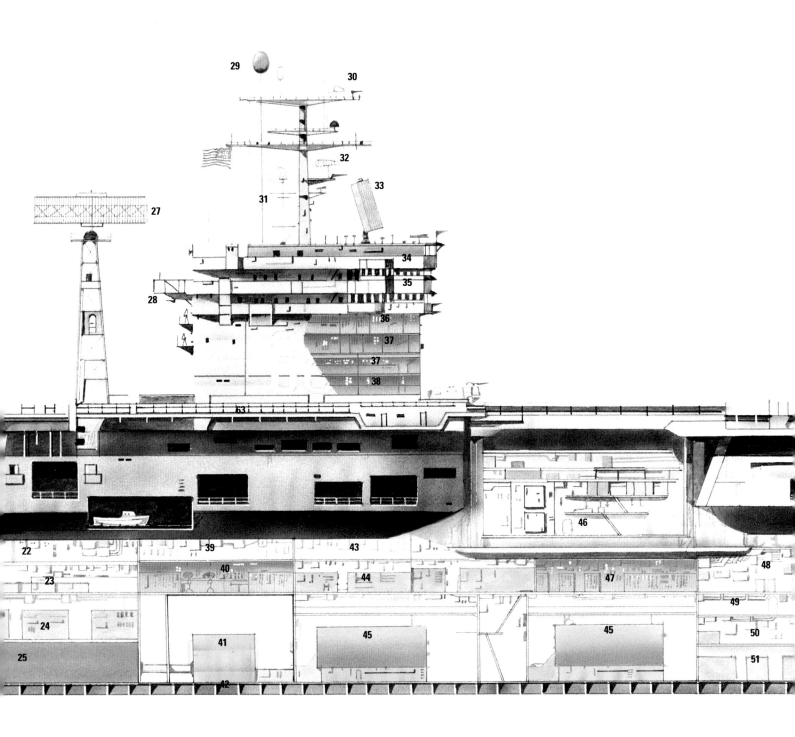

29

30

32

31

33

27

28

34

35

36

37

37

38

53

22

39

43

48

23

40

44

47

49

24

45

45

50

41

51

25

42

...ry required to fight an enemy beyond visual range, while providing ...d the effects of nuclear, biological and chemical (NBC) weapons.

Deck personnel have
dress according to th
LEFT: Red-shirted or
technicians load up
with air-to-air missil
Already in place is a
AIM-9 Sidewinder, v
the trolley carries A
Sparrows. The Sidew
short-range infra-re
(heat-seeking) weap
the Sparrow is a me
radar homing missil
targets at up to 100k
nautical miles) away
Traffic directors wea

NIMITZ

*O*n 3 May 1975, USS Nimitz *entered service with the US Navy, becoming the world's second nuclear-powered aircraft carrier. At the same time she became the world's largest warship, taking this title from USS* Enterprise, *the world's first nuclear carrier. With a population of 6,000, a library, a supermarket and her own TV and radio stations,* Nimitz *is like a city afloat. But she is also a fearsome adversary, with an air wing of almost 90 of the most advanced carrier-borne aircraft in service.*

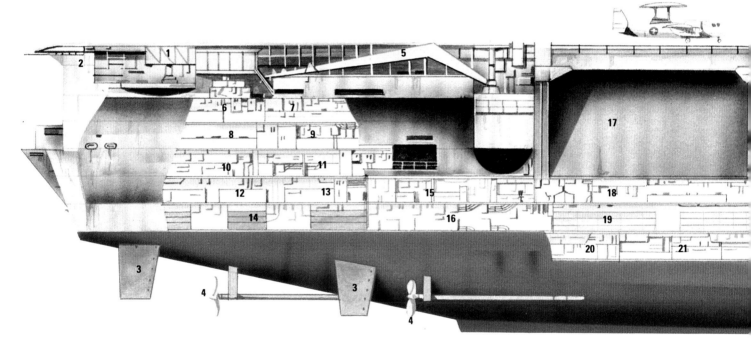

1.	Deck guard	17.	Lift
2.	MK 29 BPDMS missile launcher	18.	Maintenance
3.	Rudder	19.	Aviation stores
4.	Screw	20.	Access to shafts
5.	Crane	21.	Aircraft spares
6.	Crew quarters	22.	Air crew
7.	Aft stores control	23.	Air crew canteen
8.	Crew canteen	24.	Dynamo/Control
9.	Control centre for crane	25.	Aviation fuel
10.	Machine room	26.	Barge
11.	Stores control	27.	Surface radar
12.	Crew	28.	Deck signal lights
13.	Connecting corridor	29.	Top scan radar
14.	Ship's stores	30.	Surface radar back up
15.	Machine room	31.	Sky search radar/Missile control
16.	Dynamo room	32.	SPS10 radar

RIGHT: When th
carrier is opera
the command p
not the bridge, v
is situated in th
island and is the
too exposed, bu
darkened, elect
environment of
combat informa
center (CIC). Thi
deep in the inte
the ship, and co
all the electroni
protection from

FLASH

- *Long Beach* is the only ship in her class. She is 219.9 metres (721ft 4in) long, has a beam of 22.3 metres (73ft) and draws 9.1 metres (30ft) of water. Her displacement is 15,540 tons light and 17,524 tons full load. The ship's complement is 65 officers and 893 men; she can also accommodate 45 Marines and a flag staff of 10 officers and 58 men.

- The vessel is powered by two Westinghouse 1W pressurised water reactors linked to two General Electric turbines that can generate 80,000 horsepower. *Long Beach* has two shafts and a top speed of 30 knots.

- The 127mm (5in) guns can fire 15 rounds per minute to a range of 17km (9nm) in surface-to-surface mode, and in AA mode they have a similar rate of fire to a range of 11km (5.7nm).

- The crew live in a temperature-controlled environment. Other home comforts include daily newspapers and film showings, a tailor, barber and ice-cream bar!

45. Auxiliary command centre
46. Engineers' control centre
47. Engineers' quarters
48. Laundry
49. Gangway
50. Heavy stores
51. Sick bay
52. Fresh water tank
53. Missile magazine
54. Conveyor belt to convey missile to launcher
55. Missile launcher MK 13
56. Main missile magazine
57. Auxiliary missile magazine
58. Rack for moving up missiles to main magazine
59. Missile control centre

60. Doors to magazine
61. Crew
62. Breakwater
63. Anchor
64. Forward hawser hole
65. Sonar
66. SPS 49 air defence control radar
67. Short wave radio aerial
68. Radio signal collector
69. Air search sound sensor/Countermeasure set
70 SPS 55 control radar for forward missiles
71 SPS 48 C navigation/sea search radar
72 SPG 55 A air/surface search and control radar for forward missiles

LONG BEACH

*D*uring the 1950s and 1960s, when nuclear power seemed to be a source of limitless cheap energy, the US Navy planned that all its capital ships would one day be nuclear powered, reducing fuel bills and increasing their range and endurance infinitely at a single stroke. Before too long it became apparent that even if the project were feasible, it would be ruinously expensive, even for the richest country in the world, and it was quietly shelved, save for submarines and the biggest ships – the fleet carriers. But some smaller nuclear-powered ships were built, and continue in service, and the first and largest of those was USS Long Beach, *pennant number CGN9. The illustration shows* Long Beach *as she looked in 1983.*

1. Counter (stern)
2. Aft hawser housing
3. Rudder
4. Screw (twin)
5. Helicopter landing deck
6. Harpoon launcher MK 141
7. 20mm (0.7in) MK 15 Phalanx close-in weapons system (rapid-fire machine guns)
8. Liferafts
9. Ship's launch
10. Ship's stores
11. Cold storage
12. Machine shop
13. Flight deck machine shop
14. Main pump room
15. Turbines
16. Ventilator
17. Crew's mess deck
18. Walkway over boiler room
19. Boiler room
20. Double bottom
21. 127mm (5in) gun turret
22. Gun cradle (mount)

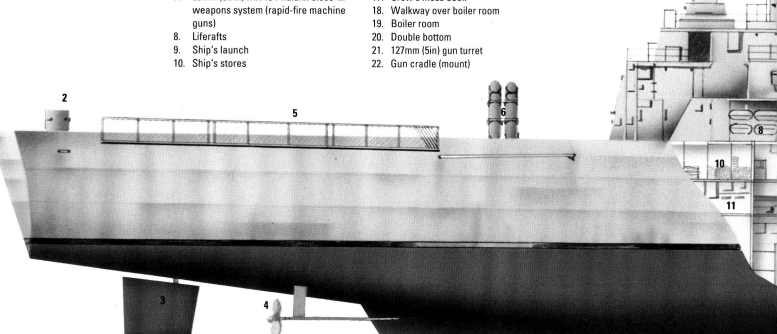

FLASH

- *Nimitz* has a full-load displacement of over 89,566 tons.

- A length of 332.9m (1,093ft) and beam of 76.8m (252ft) gives *Nimitz*'s flight deck an area of around 1.82 hectares.

- Some 6,000 sail aboard *Nimitz*. These are divided more or less 60-40 between the ship's complement and the personnel of the carrier air wing respectively.

- The final bill for building *Nimitz* was 1,881 million dollars.

- The carrier's speed of over 30 knots means that she could (in theory) tow water skiers.

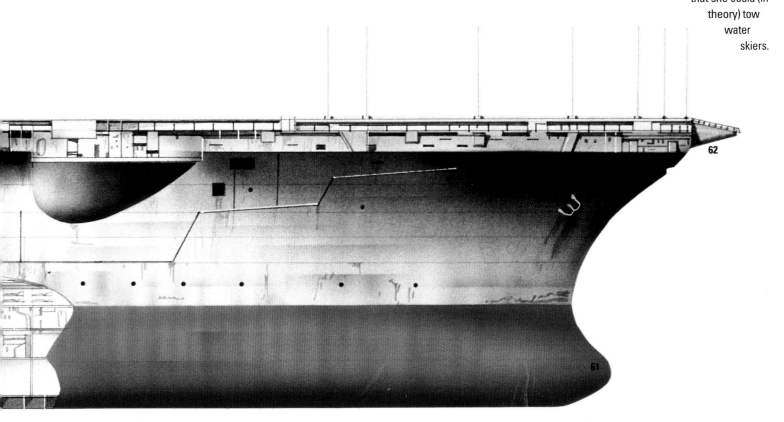

33.	Main sky search radar	49. Assembly station for damage control party
34.	Primary flight control bridge	50. Food store
35.	Navigation bridge	51. Aviation spares/magazine
36.	Ship command centre	52. Deck control landing/back up
37.	Flight control centre	53. Deck control for taking off
38.	Damage control centre	54. Fire proof doors
39.	Aviation crew	55. Crew rest area
40.	Radar control centre	56. Machine room for catapults
41.	Nuclear plant	57. Machine shop
42.	Double bottom	58. Forward assembly station for damage control/Crew quarters
43.	Deck crew quarters	59. Aviation spares/repairs
44.	Deck machine spares	60. Magazines
45.	Engine room	61. Sonar
46.	Hangar	62. Catapult launch guard
47.	Sonar control centre	63. Self inflatable life boats
48.	Air conditioning plant	64. Wireless aerials

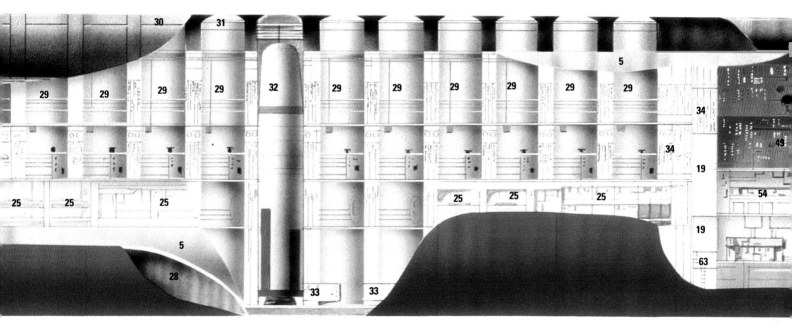

37. Observation periscope	49. Missile control centre	61. Chief petty officers' quarters
38. Attack periscope	50. Missile data base	62. Main machine room
39. Snorkel	51. Stores/Spares for computers	63. Access to battery compartment
40. Surface radar	52. Computer room	64. Battery compartment
41. Navigation light/Identification beacon	53. Food store	65. Torpedo control room
42. Radio antenna mast	54. Galley	66. Torpedo room with reloads
43. Bridge	55. Crew dining area	67. Torpedo tubes
44. Hydroplane	56. Lounge	68. Forward trim tank
45. Access tube to bridge	57. Wells for housing lowered periscopes	69. Conformal sonar
46. Command centre	58. Ship's office	70. Torpedo tube cover
47. Sonar room	59. Lobby	71. Bow hydrophone array
48. Radio room	60. Wardroom	72. Bow sonar array

RIGHT: Kirov's pyramid-like superstructure, seen here from the starboard side, bristles with sensors. On the far left is the Kite Screech main armament gun control radar, while above and to the right of that, looking a little like a space capsule, is one of the two Top Dome SA-N-6 control radars. In the centre of the picture, atop the main section of the conical mast, is the Top Steer air/sea surveillance radar.

RIGHT: A view forward along the deck of the USS Ohio, showing the open missile launch tubes. Earlier US missile submarines carried 16 missiles, the Ohios carry 24 and their tubes also have a larger diameter so that they can fire the Trident II D-5.

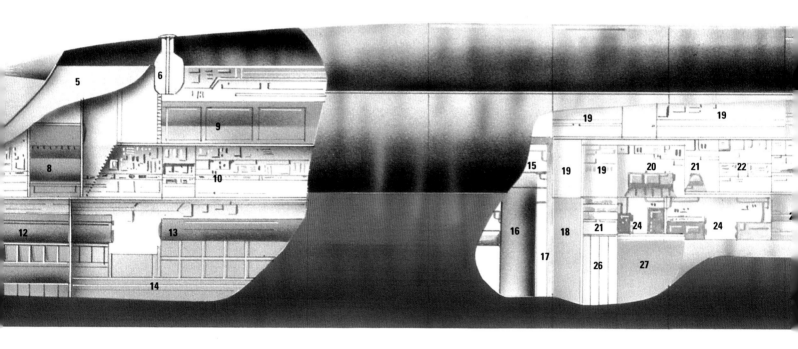

1. Screw	13. Main engine	25. Crew quarters
2. Rudder	14. Noise isolation raft	26. Midships trim tank
3. Stern hydrophone array	15. Nuclear reactor room	27. Fresh water tank
4. Outer hull casing	16. Nuclear reactor	28. Main ballast tanks
5. Inner hull	17. Insulation wall	29. Missile tube
6. Emergency escape compartment	18. Machinery lubrication oil tank	30. Outer lid to missile tube
7. Auxiliary control console	19. Companionway	31. Inner lid to missile tube
8. Condenser	20. Engineers' repair shop	32. Trident missile
9. Generators	21. Engineers' stores	33. Compressed air store (to launch missile)
10. Manoeuvring room	22. Pharmacy	34. Repeat consoles
11. Aft ballast tank	23. Sick bay	35. Navigation centre
12. Thrust block	24. Auxiliary machine room	36. Fin

OHIO

*T*he nuclear-powered Ohio class are the West's largest and most advanced missile submarines and were developed to carry the Trident submarine launched ballistic missile (SLBM), the successor to Poseidon. Their great size is linked to their need for stealth, as the plans for the new class called for expensive new noise-reduction features to be introduced. In an effort to make these improvements more cost-effective, it was decided to raise the number of missiles carried from 16 to 24. This brought a concomitant increase in the overall size of the boat to the extent that the Ohios are twice the size of the US Navy's previous class of missile submarines, the Lafayettes.

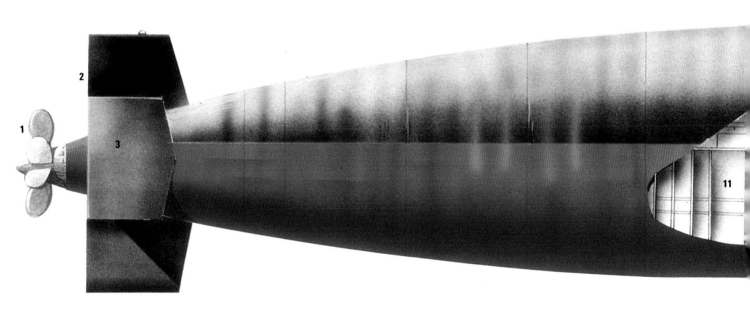

FLASH

• The Kirovs are big: 248 metres (813ft 6in) long, with a beam of 28 metres (91ft 8in), and a full-load displacement of 23,400 tons. Crew numbers around 800.

• The Kirovs are fitted with a hybrid powerplant. Known as CONAS (COmbined Nuclear And Steam), it consists of two pressurised-water reactors plus two oil-fired boilers that superheat the steam the reactors produce. This plant is linked to two sets of turbines, which supply 120,000shp to two propellers. Using nuclear plant alone the Kirovs can maintain a constant cruising speed of 24 knots, while by using nuclear and steam power together, the ships are good for 33 knots.

• Only *Kirov* carries the SS-N-14; the others have enhanced air-defence capability and carry SA-N-9 missiles. Also, instead of two single 100mm (3.9in) guns they have two 130mm (5.1in) in a twin mounting.The latter units also have a combined gun/missile, rather than gun-only, CIWS.

.   Turbines
.   Nuclear reactors (in casing)
.   Shafts for reactor removal as needed
.   Funnel uptake
.   Damage control monitoring
.   Electricians' workshop
.   Engineers' stores
.   Fresh water
.   Radio aerials
.   'Round House' TACAN tracking antenna (for

helicopter control)
40. 'Top Pair' 3-D air surveillance radar
41. Sound sensors
42. Listening devices
43. 'New Bell' type ESM radome (surface defence)
44. 'Punch Bowl' satcom antenna
45. Navigation room/Control centre
46. Bridge
47. 'Palm Frond' navigation radar
48. 'Pop Group' tracking and guidance system

49. Life rafts
50. SS-N-19 Cruise missile system
51. SA-N-6 vertical launch anti-ship missile system
52. SS-N-14 anti-submarine weapon system
53. Cover to magazine for SS-N-14 missiles
54. Chaff dispensers
55. Anchor port
56. LF hull-mounted sonar

56

KIROV

Designated a missile cruiser (RKR – *Raketnyy Kreyser*) by the Soviets when she appeared, Kirov was massively larger at 27,560 tonnes than the previous class in that category, the Kresta I class (5,900 tonnes). It has been suggested that this increase in size was necessary to provide the ship with the stamina, communications and firepower to be able to operate effectively where an enemy's air and sea capability might be strong; that is, away from Soviet home waters – in the GIUK gap, for example. It is believed Kirov and her sisters were intended to act as flagships for independent battle groups or as escorts to the Soviet carrier/guided missile cruisers of the Kiev class.

RIGHT: A stern view of Kirov, showing (from the stern) the helicopter pad, two pairs of CIWSs on platforms, and two 100mm (3.9in) dual-purpose guns. The door in the transom leads to the towed variable depth sonar housing.

CENTRE RIGHT: The foredeck of a Kirov-class ship. The heavy hatches to the right of the picture are the SS-N-19 vertical launch silos. Just forward of these are the VLSs for SA-N-6 'Grumbles'. Two CIWSs can be seen on the platform on the far side of the deck.

1. Stern door (shown open) for trailing sonar
2. LF variable-depth towed sonar
3. Rudder
4. Kamov KA 25 Hormone helicopter
5. ADGM 630 30mm (1.1in) Gatling CIWS
6. Aircraft spares
7. Hangar
8. Lift
9. Screws (one each side)
10. Lift machinery
11. 100mm (3.9in) dual-purpose automatic gun
12. Continuous belt feed hoist
13. Magazine racks
14. Ship's stores
15. Flight officer's control centre
16. 'Kite Screech' gunfire control for 100mm (3.9in) guns
17. 'Top Dome' missile fire control for SA-N-6
18. RBU-100 multibarrel ASW rocket launcher
19. Blast shield
20. 'Base Tilt' gunfire control for 30mm (1.1in) Gatling guns
21. 'Tin Man' optic rangefinder
22. 'Top Steer' surveillance radar
23. Vee-tube HF antenna (for guiding friendly aircraft)
24. Air intakes
25. 533mm (20.9in) TRM-57 ASW torpedo tubes
26. Cold store
27. Spare torpedo stowage
28. Engineers' control centre
29. Reduction gear

FLASH

• Though not as large as the Russian Typhoon class, *Ohio* is still an enormous submarine. She is 18,750 tons submerged, compared with 1,212 tons submerged for a World War II German Type IXC long-range U boat. To make another comparison, *Ohio* and her sisters are only nine metres (29ft 5in) shorter than the aircraft carrier *Giuseppe Garibaldi* and surfaced have 1.6 times her displacement.

• The Ohio-class submarines are nuclear powered. Steam produced by the S8G nuclear reactor drives electrical turbo-generators. These in turn power the electric motor that turns the single propeller shaft.

• In addition to submarine detection sonars, the Ohio class are equipped with a BQR-19 mast-mounted active side-looking navigation sonar for bottom-mapping, a BPS-15A surface search radar, a WLR-8(V)5 electronic signal monitoring (ESM) array, and two periscopes.

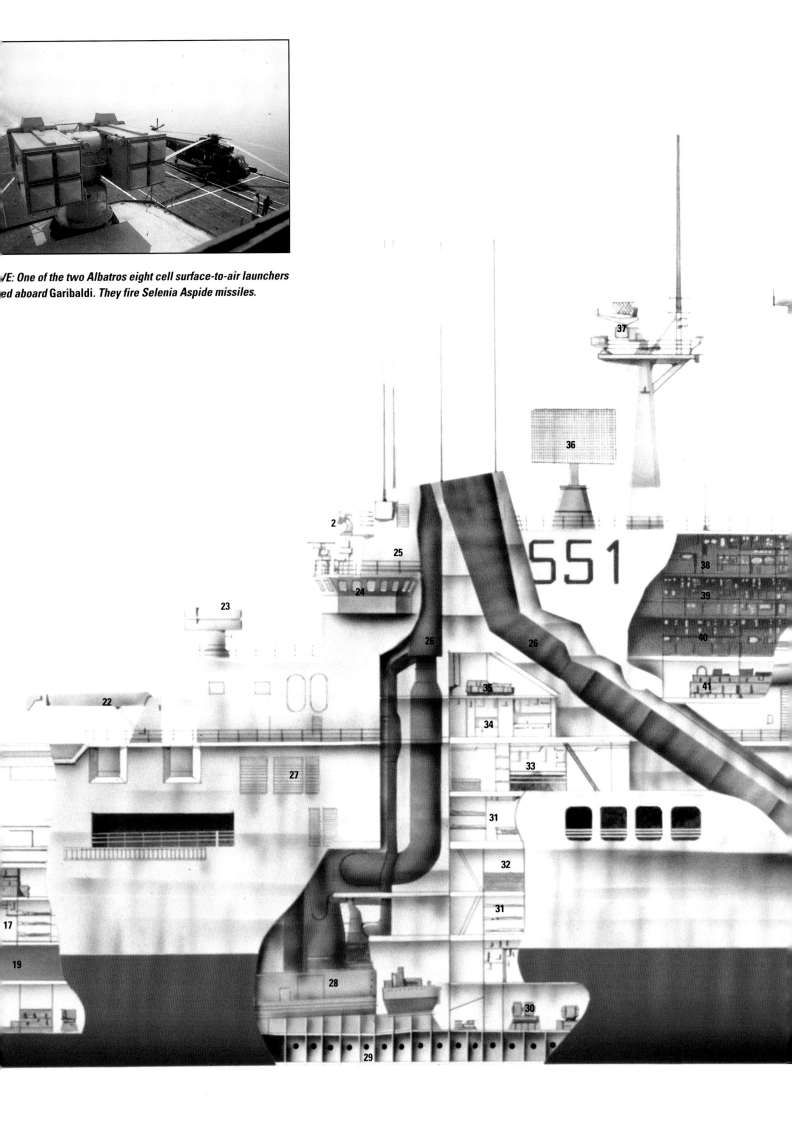

VE: One of the two Albatros eight cell surface-to-air launchers ed aboard Garibaldi. *They fire Selenia Aspide missiles.*

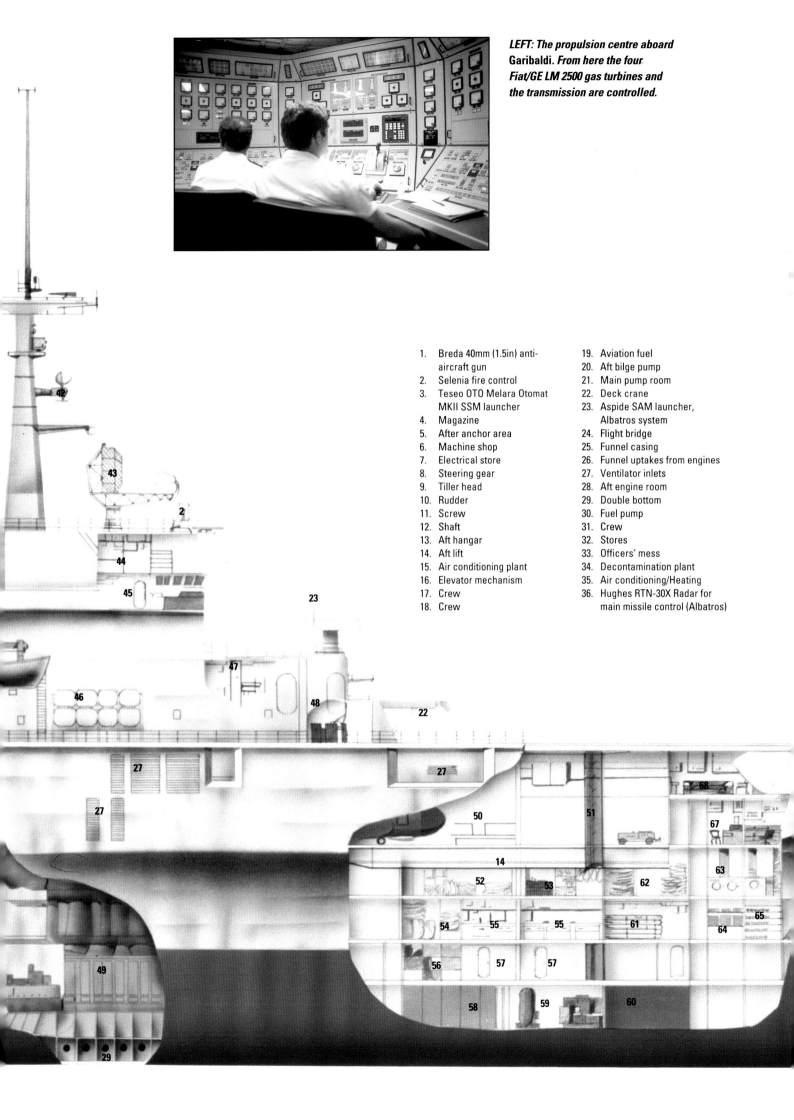

LEFT: The propulsion centre aboard Garibaldi. From here the four Fiat/GE LM 2500 gas turbines and the transmission are controlled.

1. Breda 40mm (1.5in) anti-aircraft gun
2. Selenia fire control
3. Teseo OTO Melara Otomat MKII SSM launcher
4. Magazine
5. After anchor area
6. Machine shop
7. Electrical store
8. Steering gear
9. Tiller head
10. Rudder
11. Screw
12. Shaft
13. Aft hangar
14. Aft lift
15. Air conditioning plant
16. Elevator mechanism
17. Crew
18. Crew
19. Aviation fuel
20. Aft bilge pump
21. Main pump room
22. Deck crane
23. Aspide SAM launcher, Albatros system
24. Flight bridge
25. Funnel casing
26. Funnel uptakes from engines
27. Ventilator inlets
28. Aft engine room
29. Double bottom
30. Fuel pump
31. Crew
32. Stores
33. Officers' mess
34. Decontamination plant
35. Air conditioning/Heating
36. Hughes RTN-30X Radar for main missile control (Albatros)

1. Screw
2. Tail
3. Drive shaft
4. Inner hull
5. Reduction gear
6. Electric motor room
7. Control room for engines
8. Outer hull
9. Escape hatch
10. Diesel engine room
11. Exhaust piping
12. Compressed air tanks
13. Air conditioning plant
14. Officers' cabins
15. Corridor
16. Wardroom
17. Store lading hatch
18. Radio room
19. Electrical room
20. Stores
21. Cold store
22. Galley
23. Chief engineer's office
24. Fuel tank
25. Access to batteries
26. Batteries
27. Double bottom
28. Fin casing
29. Snorkel
30. Radio mast
31. Radar
32. Short-range periscope
33. Electronic counter-measures mast
34. Long-range periscope
35. Bridge
36. Navigation light
37. Hydroplanes
38. Access to bridge
39. Fire and diving control
40. Antenna wells (for periscopes and masts)
41. Compass room
42. Petty officers' mess
43. Crew's mess
44. Sonar room
45. Torpedo room
46. 'Harpoon' missile
47. Mk 48 torpedo
48. Torpedo tube (533mm)
49. Ballast tank
50. Trim tank
51. Anchor chain well
52. Outer torpedo tube door
53. Passive (defensive) sonar

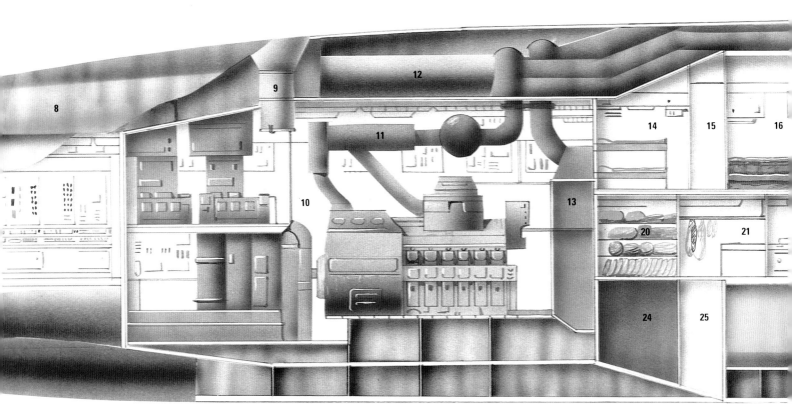

ZEELEEUW

*A*lthough Holland has less than 500 kilometres (310 miles) of coastline, its strategic importance in naval terms *considerable, for it controls the mouth of the Rhine, as well as having the continent's biggest seaport at Rotterdam. T Dutch have always been a seafaring nation, and during the 20th century have developed a considerable reputation submariners. The first post-World War II Dutch submarines, the four Dolfijn class boats, featured a unique triangu arrangement of pressure tubes which maximised their internal volume while allowing them to dive deeper. The newest cl of boats, led by Zeeleeuw, have improved on diving depths still further, and are as good as any submarines in the world.*

LEFT: *A Zeeleeuw-class submarin on the surface. A distinguishing feature of this type of submarine is the X-plane tail rudder, two fins of which can be seen above the water. Unlike the conventional cruciform tail surface, the X-plane allows for finer control of depth and bearing, and simplifies 'bottoming' and mooring.*

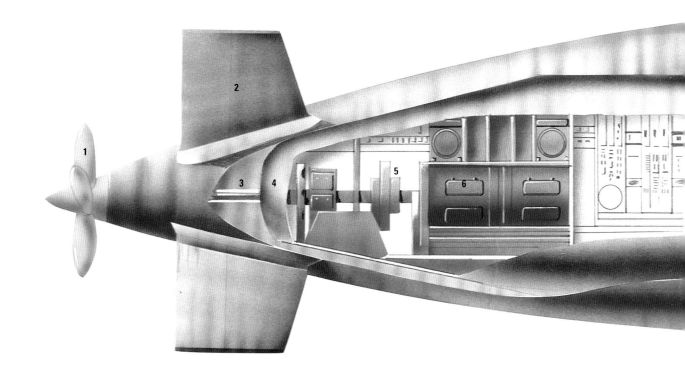

FLASH

• The present *Giuseppe Garibaldi*, launched on 4 June 1983, is the fourth Italian warship to bear the name. The first was an auxiliary frigate launched on 28 January 1860; the second was an armoured cruiser launched on 29 June 1899; the third was a light cruiser launched on 21 April 1934.

• *Giuseppe Garibaldi* is 180 metres (590ft) long, has a beam of 23.5 metres (77ft), draws 6.7 metres (22ft) of water, and displaces 13,287 tons at full load.

• The carrier's full complement consists of 550 officers and men, plus a further 230 air wing personnel; a flag staff of 45 may also be accommodated.

• *Giuseppe Garibaldi* (13,287 tons/30 knots) is similar in type to the Royal Navy's Invincible class (19,193/28) and the Spanish Navy's *Principe de Asturias* (15,945/26). All are designed to carry helicopters and V/STOL aircraft and none have catapults.

nia short range surface
r
n radar room
mand centre
ondary radar room
ward working area
A MM/SPS-702 surface
ction
nia RAN 3L MM/SPS-
medium-range air radar
erve store for chaff
ge
saving equipment
azine and re-loading
for Aspide missiles
e engine
fighting store
e hangar
munition hoist
rgency supplies
rigeration plant

54. Flour store
55. Galley
56. Food store
57. Corridor
58. Freshwater
59. Pump room
60. Fuel (diesel)
61. Magazine
62. Linen store
63. Laundry
64. Ship's stores
65. Wine store
66. Wine hoist
67. Office
68. Crew mess
69. Anchor deck
70. Capstan
71. Chain locker
72. Anchor
73. Sonar bulge

GIUSEPPE GARIBALDI

Giuseppe Garibaldi *is a valuable asset to NATO's Mediterranean naval capability. She is one of the most formidable ships in any European fleet. Her aircrafts' contribution to the maintenance of air superiority, her protective weapons fit and her capacity to mount amphibious landing operations fit her to act as the command and control centre for an entire combined task force – whether in the purely military sense or in her envisaged secondary role in disaster relief operations.*

FLASH

• *Zeeleeuw and* her three sisters are 67.75 metres (222ft) long with a maximum beam of 8.4 metres (27ft 5in). Their submerged displacement of 2,755 tons puts them among the biggest diesel-electric attack submarines (SSKs) in the world.

• As well as British-designed 2026 towed array sonar, the Zeeleeuw-class submarines have the French medium-frequency 'Octopus' hull-mounted active/passive search and attack sonar system and ZW 07 I-band surface search radar, which is also used for navigation purposes.

• Maximum service depth of the submarines is 300 metres (984ft), although their pressure depth (the actual maximum depth to which they can sink and survive) remains undisclosed.

• Each Zeeleeuw-class submarine cost around $210 million to build.

LEFT: One of the two periscopes and the screens for the Gipsy-system (Integrated Information and Presentation System) in the command centre aboard Zeeleeuw. *BELOW: The Zeeleeuw-class submarines are larger versions of the previous Zwaardvis class, with greater diving depth and improved systems. Here the Zwaardvis-class submarine* Tijgerhaai *(S807), laid down in 1966 and commissioned in October 1972, travels on the surface in rough sea.*